The Bible and People
of Other Faiths

The Bible
and People of
Other Faiths

S. Wesley Ariarajah

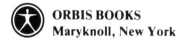

ORBIS BOOKS
Maryknoll, New York

First published as No. 26 in the Risk book series, copyright © 1985 by the World Council of Churches, 150 route de Ferney, 1211 Geneva 20, Switzerland

U.S. edition published 1989 by Orbis Books, Maryknoll, NY 10545
Produced in the United States of America

Library of Congress Cataloging-in-Publication Data

Ariarajah, S. Wesley.
    The Bible and people of other faiths / S. Wesley Ariarajah.
        p.   cm.
    Reprint. Originally published: Geneva : World Council of Churches, c1985. Originally published in series: The Risk book series : no. 26.
    ISBN 0-88344-272-8
    1. Bible—Criticism, interpretation, etc.   2. Christianity and other religions.   3. Jesus Christ—Person and offices. I. Title.
[BS511.2.A62   1989]
261.2—dc19   88-26773
                                                                              CIP

TO
SHYAMALA

Table of contents

Foreword

The Bible is the record of a great dialogue. God's word – which both expresses and enacts the divine will – created the whole universe. This same creating, judging and promising word/event of God shaped the world of nations, one particular people, the person of Jesus, and the early church.

To examine what dialogue means does indeed belong to the core of biblical studies. But it needs to be admitted that the biblical story concentrates mainly on God's dialogue with just one people, the people of Israel, and – through Christ – with the early church. It tells us little about the way in which other peoples, living in other cultures and epochs, were challenged by God and how they responded. In the biblical record nothing is explicitly spelled out about what we might learn from such great teachers as Gautama Buddha or from such formidable prophets like Mohammed. To reflect biblically about God and the people of other faiths is therefore a difficult and risky enterprise.

One could easily make a strong case showing that according to the Bible God has nothing to do with people of other faiths. In order to support this view one would simply have to pick out of their context passages such as Hosea's condemnation of Canaanite fertility cults or some exclusivist sayings of Jesus in John's Gospel. By using similar proof-texting the opposite affirmation also could be made, namely that God has much to teach us through God's presence among people of other faiths. In order to "prove" this, one could point to the biblical Wisdom literature, with its amazing openness to what can be learned from Egyptian or Mesopotamian wisdom. Further support could be found in the first part of the prologue to John's Gospel, in speculations on the "cosmic Christ" or the "Christ incognito" based on passages in Colossians and Ephesians.

The author of this study has rightly rejected such a proof-texting misuse of the Bible. He attempts to listen to the whole biblical message. On the basis of this he thinks biblically on a highly controversial question which is crucial for our time and for which no ready-made answers are available in the Bible. In the course of it the author must state his own understanding on how the Bible is to be interpreted. He uses insights gained in a series of study conferences whose reports are collected and introduced in the volume *The Bible: its Authority and Interpretation in the Ecumenical Movement* (WCC, Geneva 1980; cf.

especially the 1971 report on "The Authority of the Bible" and the 1977 report on "The Significance of the Old Testament in its Relation to the New").

What, then, can we learn from this exploration on the Bible and people of other faiths? First of all, many of the critical questions which constantly arise in connection with the dialogue between Christians and people of other faiths are honestly taken up here and discussed in the light of the biblical message. Secondly, the author shows convincingly that among the variety of biblical traditions there is one which not only legitimizes such a dialogue but challenges us to enter into it. Thirdly, here are important biblical insights about the theological presuppositions and the necessary spiritual attitudes for such a dialogue.

No final answers are proposed and readers are challenged to join an ongoing exploration. Some will disagree with the kind of biblical interpretation followed in this study. Others will miss important aspects of the theme, for instance a discussion of the relationship between the Bible and the scriptures of other faiths, or the discussion of the question whether God does not have a continuing special relationship with the Jewish people and, if so, what it implies for the Jewish-Christian dialogue. Still others may want to emphasize parts of the Bible which they consider to be especially relevant for God's relationship with people of other faiths and are not sufficiently dealt with in these chapters, as for instance the biblical Wisdom literature.

The scope of the theme taken up in this book is indeed much larger than this small volume suggests. Personally I do not know of any study which explores this theme in such a clear, concise and competent way as is done by Wesley Ariarajah. I therefore heartily recommend the reading and discussion of this book.

HANS-RUEDI WEBER

Introduction

Asia is the home of many religious traditions. Many of the great religions of the world have grown out of the Asian people's attempts over the centuries to grasp the meaning of life and human destiny. Dialogue has always been part and parcel of the Asian understanding of religious life and discipline.

When the Asia-Pacific Region of the World Student Christian Federation (WSCF) asked me to write a book on dialogue, what they were looking for was something that would help an average Christian to relate to people who live by other faith convictions. How can Christians in today's world live and witness to Hindus, Buddhists, Muslims and other religious communities in an attitude of dialogue? How can this be done without denying one's own faith, without even hiding it? Is it possible to be in dialogue and still remain a convinced Christian?

Much has been written during the last decade on the meaning and practice of interfaith dialogue, the need for it and the limits of it. An interested student can without difficulty find sufficient material to begin a serious reflection on the subject.

In responding to the WSCF request, therefore, I have chosen to deal with what in some ways is a more difficult subject, namely "The Bible and People of other Faiths". This subject should be of interest to a much larger constituency than the WSCF had in mind, and hence this joint WCC-WSCF (Asia-Pacific) publication. I am grateful to friends in both these organizations for their encouragement.

Why the Bible?

Much of the criticism levelled against dialogue is claimed to be based on the Bible. "The Bible says that Jesus is the way, the truth and the life," a friend told me the other day, "and the only way you can continue the dialogue programme is by denying this unequivocal witness of the Bible to who Jesus is, and why he was sent by the Father."

Is this indeed true? Is the Bible not supportive of dialogue with people of other religious traditions? Is there in it a teaching on Jesus and his significance that runs contrary to the intentions of genuine dialogue?

Even though it is difficult to deal with such a subject in a small book, it is important at least to begin an exploration of this issue.

My intention is not to prove that dialogue is biblical, or that the friend who raised the question with me is wrong. I am well aware that the question arose out of a very genuine concern. It is quite understandable why people believe that the Bible is opposed to dialogue.

For many centuries the Bible itself, and particularly certain verses in the Bible which make exclusive claims for Christ, have been used in Christian teaching and preaching to show why people should become Christians, leaving behind the faiths of their ancestors. The churches in minority situations, as in Asia and in many other parts of the world, have been sustained by the belief that their life apart from the dominant culture and religious milieu is sanctioned, and even demanded, by the scripture.

Millions of Christians in Asia read the Bible daily, both as part of their personal devotion and at family prayers. Many take their Bible with them when they go to church for Sunday worship.

Large numbers of persons in many parts of the world who, for one reason or another, do not wish to display their Christian faith in public, or have chosen not to be part of the institutional structures of religion, cling to the reading of the Bible as the symbol and source of their Christian faith.

The question therefore must be faced sooner or later. And it should be faced not in the spirit of proving or disproving one's position, but in a spirit that opens up new ways of understanding and relating to the traditions handed down in scripture.

The difficulties

I must explain why this is a difficult subject to discuss. The first problem is that the Bible is not a book that deals with other faiths or with the question of dialogue with people of other faiths. In fact, in some ways, it deals with quite the opposite of dialogue. It is primarily about two of the faiths that we have today, Judaism and Christianity. In much of the material in it there is open witness offered to these two religious traditions by those who stand within them and bear testimony to their beliefs. What we have on other faiths in the Bible is therefore incidental to the major concern, which is to bear testimony to one's own faith. It is unreasonable to expect in the Bible a well-developed teaching on the faiths of others.

We must, therefore, draw out the implications of the biblical teaching, rather than look for direct guidance on dialogue.

The second major problem has to do with the question of interpretation. There is no general agreement among Christians on how the scripture is to be read and interpreted. Some would treat the Bible as the Word of God in the sense that every word written there is true and given by God. There are, however, not too many who hold this view. But there are many who insist that the Bible should not be subjected to critical methods of study. For example, the question whether the sayings attributed to Jesus in St John's Gospel were in fact said by Jesus would deeply upset them. They would argue that to say that St John's Gospel reflects the early church's beliefs about Jesus, rather than reproduce his very words, is to undermine the authority of scripture. They would not want to deal with the vastly different pictures drawn of Jesus by Mark on the one hand and John on the other, but would want to hold on to both within their overall understanding of who Jesus is.

Then there are others who make it their business to probe the scripture, in the sense of subjecting it to rigorous critical methods of study. They try to understand the life and teachings of Jesus which lie behind all that the early Christians have given us in the Bible. Here too, the Bible is taken seriously, but there is a recognition that it is written by people whose reflections are coloured by their own faith and by their own attempts to understand Christ and his significance.

It is therefore impossible to deal with the Bible in a way that is acceptable to all. I must confess that I have moved over the years from one position to another in the way I myself relate to the Bible. Therefore, even though I may now speak from the historical critical angle, I am aware of the honesty and intensity of other positions that people hold and other attitudes they have towards the Bible. It is my hope that whatever is said here comes through in a confessional rather than a dogmatic way of stating the case.

In fact, given the material that we have in the Bible, there is no argument to be won. All that one can hope to do is to show another side of the Bible that makes a clear case for a new attitude to people of other faiths. Or one would need to show why the material from scripture usually quoted against dialogue is in fact not against dialogue. This can only be done by showing the nature of the material quoted and the context in which it had been used.

The discussion, however, must focus not on isolated verses of the Bible but on the overall teaching of the Bible. Here I am firmly convinced that there is in the Bible another attitude to people of other faiths that Christians in Asia and elsewhere need to recover and celebrate. All that I hope to do is to lift this up.

In so doing I have tried, to the best of my ability, to be faithful to biblical scholarship. It is obvious, however, that in many places I have opted for one or another interpretation without adequately discussing all possible options. This is done mainly because of the constituency for which the book is being written. We have to assume that a large part of this constituency is not familiar with the debates within biblical scholarship, nor wants to be drawn into the details of them. Nor, for that matter, is the book meant for scholars. It is meant for ordinary Christians living in situations of religious pluralism, and constantly challenged to relate to people of other living faiths.

The primary purpose here is to show that some of the common assumptions about the Bible and persons of other faiths can indeed be questioned from within the Bible. It is hoped that this will kindle a desire in many to re-read the Bible in a new way and from another perspective.

The Bible and People
of Other Faiths

1. No other God

Some years ago, I served as a pastor in Kandy, a beautiful town in the central highlands of Sri Lanka. I was responsible for a weekly Bible study programme for the SCM students at the university in an adjoining town. One day we were discussing a Hindu festival that was being planned to be held on the campus. "We usually do not go to the festival," said one of the students, "because we don't worship the Hindu God." The formulation of that statement fascinated me. "Do you mean that you don't agree with the way that Hindus understand God," I asked her, "or are you saying that there is a Hindu God, different from a Christian God?" "I don't know," she said with some hesitation, aware now that I had difficulties with what she had said. "But don't the Hindus and Muslims worship their gods, but we worship the true God revealed to us in Jesus Christ?"

This indeed is the crux of the issue with regard to the Bible and people of other faiths. In one sense what my student friend said is true. There is in fact a Christian, a Hindu and a Muslim conception of God and, when worship is offered, people have a particular conception of God with which others may agree or disagree. One must say that, even within the same religion, sometimes one's own conception of God is very different from another person's. But how many gods are there in the universe and beyond it? Are there many gods to choose from? Is there room for a Christian god, a Hindu god and a Muslim god?

Beginning where it all began

The whole Bible stands on one firm foundation: there is one God, no other. Apostasy in the Bible is to believe that there are other gods, that they are real, and to worship them. The Bible therefore begins with creation, a biblical concept that is fundamental to our relationship with people of other faiths.

Significantly it is the story not of the creation of the church, or of Christians, not even of Israel, but of the cosmos: "In the beginning God created the heavens and the earth." This belief that God is the creator of everything and everybody is basic to the Bible. There is nothing that is outside God's providence; there is no life, no experience, no worship, no liberation, no salvation that can happen outside the scope of God's love and knowledge. This theme of the universal lordship of God over all creation is the resounding theme of many of the psalms: "The

world and all that is in it belong to the Lord; the earth and all
who live on it are his" (Ps. 24).

The creation psalms make the claim that all life totally and
entirely depends on this one God for its being. Psalm 104
presents this thought in beautiful poetry:

> Lord, you have made so many things!
> How wisely you have made them all!
> The earth is filled with your creatures…
> all of them depend on you
> to give them food when they need it.
> You give it to them, and they eat it;
> you provide food, and they are satisfied.
> When you turn away they are afraid;
> when you take away their breath they die
> and go back to the dust from which they came.
> But when you give them breath they are created;
> you give new life to the earth (vv. 24-30).

The basic assumption of the Bible, then, is that there is no
other provider but God – the one God – who is the creator of
everyone. People may or may not have an adequate understanding of who this God is, and their worship may or may not do
justice to their understanding of God; but ultimately they are all
provided for by this one God. Therefore, from God's side there
can only be one family, the human family.

Universal Covenant

The opening chapters of Genesis are not about any particular
groups of people but about the whole human family. In the
Bible, Adam and Eve are prototypes of every human person, of
whatever religion or race. They are created in the "image and
likeness" of God. God blessed them abundantly and assigned to
them the care of the earth.

In the same way, the tragedy of human alienation from God,
depicted in the story of Adam and Eve in the Garden of Eden, is
also a paradigm of the predicament of the whole human race. It
is meant as a story that describes the broken state of relationship
between God and every human being.

It is indeed significant that the Bible begins with the affirmation of the common humanity of all people, both in their
participation in the life of God (image) and in their state of

alienation from that source of life (in the "fall"). Even though the Bible story is only one way of describing who human beings are and how they relate to God, it is surely not without interest that the opening chapters choose to speak of the human family as a whole rather than deal with a section of it.

It does not stop there either. These chapters go on to develop the concept of God's covenant relationship with the whole human family. The Universal Covenant which God makes with Noah (ch.9) goes in fact beyond humanity to embrace all living things. It is a moving account of God's compassion for all creatures and God's decision to bless them again that they might multiply and fill the earth.

The special word "covenant", which implies mutual trust and responsibility, is used to describe the relationship between God and all of creation. It is signed and sealed, as it were, by the sign of the rainbow:

> As a sign of this everlasting covenant which I am making with all living beings, I am putting my bow in the clouds. It will be a sign of my covenant with the world... when the rainbow appears in the clouds, I will see it and remember the everlasting covenant between me and all living beings on earth... (Gen. 9:12,16).

The opening chapters of the Bible, up to Genesis 12, where God calls Abram, who was later named Abraham, are an affirmation of God's relationship with all people. The biblical story could easily have begun with chapter 12 with the call of Abraham. But there seems to be almost a conscious attempt to place the story of Israel in the broader context of God's creative, redemptive and covenant relationship with the whole of humanity and all created order.

The Chosen People

From Genesis chapter 12, however, this universal story narrows down to the story of Israel. It is important to note this, because one can never understand the Bible unless one recognizes that from this point onwards the Bible is primarily concerned with the story of Israel and not of other nations. The other nations, their histories and their faiths, are considered mainly from the standpoint of Israel. In fact the histories of great empires like those of Egypt, Assyria and Babylon are all seen from the standpoint of Israel's history and religion, and not from the perspective that God is God over all nations.

It is also important to consider some of the elements involved in this narrowing down of the scope of the Hebrew scriptures that are called "Old Testament" in the Bible used by Christians. For it has much to do with the self-understanding of the church and its relationship with people of other faiths.

Three aspects stand out. First, there are many clear passages in the Bible which say that God chose the nation of Israel to be God's own people. This is seen as a conscious choice that God makes from among all the nations. Second, there is the understanding that God made a fresh covenant with Abraham, reaffirmed many times, especially through the covenant with Moses on the basis of the Law. Third, there is also the belief that Israel is the "light to the nations", or that God will bless the nations through Israel.

The church, which grew out of Israel, inherited all these three, appropriating them as part of its understanding of the church's relationship with God. In fact the church went further than Israel and claimed that God has expressed a new preference. Thus the special scriptures of the Christians (called the New Testament) claimed that the Christians were the true Israel, God's chosen people for the new age which Jesus inaugurated. The teaching comes through in the writings of Paul, Peter and the author of the Letter to the Hebrews. "But you are the chosen race, the King's priests, the holy nation, God's own people," writes Peter to the Christians under persecution. "At one time you were not God's people, but now you are his people; at one time you did not know God's mercy, but now you have received his mercy" (1 Pet. 2:10).

The Christian community was also convinced that God has made a new covenant with the followers of Christ. That was why the Hebrew scriptures which became part of the Christian Bible were called the Old Testament, meaning the old covenant, and the Christian writings were classified as the New Testament, or new covenant. Paul argues that the old covenant, based on the Law, leads to death, and the new covenant, based on grace, leads to life (Gal. 3). He goes on further to contrast Adam with Christ. The creative order based on Adam, who was created of dust, leads to death, but the creative order based on

Christ, the new humanity, leads to life eternal (Rom. 5). Thus "if anyone is in Christ, there is a new creation" (Cor. 5).

The author of the Letter to the Hebrews takes every institution on which the life and faith of Israel is based – the temple, the sacrifice, the Law, the high priest who mediates between God and people – and attempts to show how and why the Christian community is the true Israel that has replaced the old.

The church, it is further claimed, is "the light of the nations". It is through its ministry that the nations are to taste the joy of salvation. To begin with, the claim is made for the Logos, the Word which became flesh. He is "the real light – the light that comes into the world and shines on all mankind" (John 1:9). Very soon, however, the community that accepted him as Lord and bore his name is seen as the channel, at least the agent, of salvation. This community, according to Peter, has been called "out of darkness into his own marvellous light" (1 Pet. 2:9). Paul is convinced that the ministry of reconciliation is entrusted to this community. They are now "the chosen race", "the holy nation" and "God's own people".

Does God choose nations?

The church's understanding that it is the newly chosen people has created great difficulties in its relationship with the Jewish people. St Paul in his Letter to the Romans deals with this difficulty at some length and attempts to arrive at some compromise which need not concern us at this point. But since Judaism continues to this day as a living, vital religion, and believes that the covenant which God made with Abraham, Jacob, Moses and others is valid to this day, we are faced with the anomaly of conflicting claims to the status of God's chosen people.

This is a difficult subject, and a sensitive one. Here we deal with the self-understandings of distinct religious communities which hold so much meaning for them. And yet any discussion of God and the people of other faiths cannot avoid facing this question of God's choice of peoples.

The first question, therefore, is whether God in fact chose Israel from among the nations for a special ministry and relationship. Unfortunately there can be no objective answer to this question. A Jew would have no doubt about this because that is precisely what it means to be a Jew, and their scripture bears ample testimony to it.

To a Hindu this may appear an extraordinary claim, for how can one say that God did not, or does not, choose other nations and establish special relationships with them? How does one deal with the equally strongly held convictions in the sacred scriptures of others where God is said to have revealed the divine will for them, and has asked them to be a light to the nations?

Can we therefore conclude that Israel and the church were misguided in their belief that they have a special relationship with God? Indeed we cannot. We must respect Abraham's conviction that God had called him out of Ur with a definite purpose and for a special relationship. If we have no objective evidence to confirm it, neither do we have evidence to contradict it. In the same way we cannot prove or disprove, accept or reject, Israel's belief expressed in their scriptures that they are a covenant people chosen by God. It is a self-understanding that governs the whole of the life of Israel.

Outside the context of faith, however, and the community which lives by that faith, such claims have little value or relevance. While the belief that God chooses one nation over another looks natural to Israel and to the church, a Hindu will find it difficult to accept that God can ever do such a thing. A Muslim will claim that inasmuch as the Prophet has had the latest revelation, the Qur'an now reveals the definitive will of God. Christians tend to treat the choice of the Jewish people as the preparation for the new community in Christ. What have we to say about these other claims?

God of the nations

When we return to the Bible, we do not get much help. For the Bible, as we have said, is basically the history and the celebration of the faith of the Jewish and Christian peoples. It reflects and reinforces their self-understanding.

A closer look at the Bible, however, also reveals a parallel tradition. There are a number of passages in scripture which continue the theme of creation even within the context of Israel's self-understanding. These suggest that Israel's own self-perception cannot be used as a comment on God's relationship with other nations, whether in love or in judgment. Such verses are few and far between, but they certainly throw some light on our concern.

The opening chapter of Amos, for example, puts all nations, including Israel, under God's judgment.

> The Lord says, the people of Damascus have sinned again and again, and for this I will punish them...
>
> The people of Edom have sinned again and again, and for this I will certainly punish them...
>
> The people of Moab have sinned again and again, and for this I will punish them...
>
> The people of Israel have sinned again and again, and for this I will certainly punish them.

Amos goes much further in chapter 9:

> The Lord says, "People of Israel, I think as much of the people of Sudan as I do of you. I brought the Philistines from Crete and the Syrians from Kir, just as I brought you from Egypt" (Amos 9:7).

It is of course impossible to argue from a single verse in the Bible that there is a clear teaching to the effect that God cares for all nations as he does for Israel, and that he brings all of them out of oppression as he did Israel when they were slaves in Egypt. But Amos's message is indicative of a theme that is in fact present within the Hebrew Bible more often than is realized.

The books of Isaiah take up the theme of the universal lordship of God over all nations. Here in many passages the prophet looks forward to the time when harmony will be restored to all nations and indeed to the whole of creation. In chapter 19, for example, the Lord God proclaims himself not so much as the God of Israel as the God of the nations. Egypt and Assyria, the bitter enemies of Israel, are seen to belong to God as much as Israel. There is a promise that God will do for Egypt all that he did for Israel, including the people's redemption from oppression:

> When the time comes, there will be an altar of the Lord in the land of Egypt and a stone pillar dedicated to him at the Egyptian border. They will be the symbols of the Lord Almighty's presence in Egypt. When the people there are oppressed and call out to the Lord for help, he will send someone to rescue them. The Lord will reveal himself to the Egyptian people and they will acknowledge and worship him and bring him sacrifices and offerings (19:19-21).

The passage goes even further to point out that God will establish this relationship not through Israel but directly, and that Israel itself will be just one among the nations that God loves.

> When the time comes, there will be a highway between Egypt and Assyria. The people of those two countries will travel to and fro between them, and the two nations will worship together. When that time comes, Israel will rank with Egypt and Assyria, and these three nations will be a blessing to all the world. The Lord Almighty will bless them and say: "I will bless you Egypt, my people; you Assyria, whom I created; and you Israel, my chosen people" (19:23-25).

The prophets thus saw God as the Lord of all nations. When Israel overcame other nations, of course it was interpreted as victory given to them by the Lord. But when they were defeated and taken captives, they interpreted it not so much as a victory God gave to other nations as the punishment God meted out to them for the sins of the nation. The logic, however, leads to the conclusion that God is the Lord of the history of all nations.

The outstanding acknowledgment of this is seen in Isaiah 45 where Cyrus the king of Persia is called the "chosen" of the Lord:

> The Lord has chosen Cyrus to be King!
> He has appointed him to conquer nations;
> he sends him to strip kings of their power;
> the Lord will open the gates of the cities for him (45:1).

There are many similar passages in the Bible which celebrate the theme of the universal Lordship of God over all peoples and nations.

It is obvious that such verses cannot serve as conclusive arguments. For there are many other verses in the Bible that can be cited to show that Israel had a special relationship with God which was not shared by other nations. There are passages that appear exclusive, and judgmental of all other nations.

The point we are making here, however, is a different one. The Bible, especially the part that is common to Jews and Christians, is the scripture of the Jewish people. It is based on the self-understanding of the Jewish people as the people of God. It is literature and history interpreted and written within that self-understanding. Its truth and validity can never be tested or proved outside the context of that faith and self-understanding. The people of the Hebrew part of our scripture may even have thought of their choice among nations as an objective truth. And yet the outsider can view it only as a subjective experience. That experience cannot be denied, but it has no meaning for those who are not part of it.

The biblical verses we have been looking at are not quoted to disprove that self-understanding, but to show that Israel kept the concept of chosenness within God's universal relationship with all nations. We should remember that it is not outsiders, but Israel's own prophets who remind the nation of its own conviction that God rules over all people.

The passages also show that Israel constantly kept under review its own self-understanding as the chosen people. They indicate that God's calling of Israel is not so much to be his "favourites" as to fulfill God's own righteousness. It is certainly revealing that Israel's own traditions kept these themes alive within the scripture. However few the passages may be, it is important that they are there, and they should inform our understanding of the Bible as a whole.

We must now return to where we began this chapter, to the theme of creation.

If God is the creator of the whole universe, and its provider, what does it say about those of other faiths? If God has indeed made a universal covenant with the whole creation (in Noah), does God then go back on that covenant?

The Christian understanding that the new covenant abrogates, supersedes, or "dates" the earlier ones as "old" is a curious one. It is an attempt to "update" God who is beyond time and in whom time itself has meaning. Does God go back on the covenants he makes?

The logical implication of the biblical teaching of God as creator is that God indeed is the creator of all people, whether Christian or Hindu, Jew or Muslim. The biblical teaching that God is the provider simply means that there is no other God who provides; it is God the creator who provides for all living beings. All beings live and move and have their being in that God. There is no Christian God, Hindu God or Muslim God; there can only be Christian, Hindu and Muslim understandings of God – or the denial that God exists by those who do not believe in God. The biblical teaching is that there are no two gods, only God. There can be no other god.

This point needs to be emphasized over and over again because the university student who talked of a "Hindu God" is not untypical of the average Christian in Asia. While the average Christian in Asia would affirm, at the intellectual and doctrinal level, that there is one God, there is a functional polytheism that pervades the Asian Christian way of dealing with people of other faiths. One only needs to probe at some depth, as I have done a number of times, to discover that it is the Christian, and not the Hindu as is often claimed, who is the polytheist. For while a Hindu will have no problem in affirming that we worship the one God, the Christian will have considerable difficulty. Somehow God in the Christian mind has become "a tribal God". Christians have enormous difficulty in accepting that the Hindu, the Buddhist and the communist are in fact created and sustained by God the creator to whom the Bible bears witness.

Let me anticipate a possible misunderstanding here. What we have said so far about the implications of the biblical understanding of God as creator does not mean that all religions are the same. Nor does it warrant the assertion that "all religions lead to the same goal". No, it does not mean that people have the same or equally valid understandings of the nature of the ultimate reality in which they have their being. Not all religions have equally challenging ways of describing what one's faith in God involves for human relationships and social ordering. Not all religions show us how to relate to these in a way that really fulfills the purposes of creation. Religions differ. They are not the same. They are not equally valid nor equally true. But while they are different, each holds enormous validity and truth for its own believers. And all of them have in them their demonic elements as well.

But what the above consideration does mean is that there is no person, no history, no culture, no spirituality that is outside God's creation and providence. What it does mean is that all yearnings for God, all attempts to know and love God, however right or wrong, appropriate or inappropriate, happen within God's providence. A radical recovery of God as creator means that my Hindu or Buddhist neighbour, whether I like or dislike the way he or she worships God, is still the child of God. God is as much his or her creator as mine. For there is no other God but the God who is the source of all being.

It is in this context that we must look at the doctrine of election, or the understanding that one or another religious group has that it is "chosen" by God. Such a self-understanding is valid only insofar as it does not violate the doctrine of God as creator. Israel's or the church's understanding that they are the chosen people is only a comment about themselves and not about others. The claim in Amos that the Lord brought "the Philistines from Crete and the Syrians from Kir" and the affirmation in Isaiah that "Israel will rank with Egypt and Assyria" are a corrective to the possible conclusion that God has abandoned the other nations or does not listen to their cries.

Christian theology should allow God to be God; it should not own God, as we own a piece of private property. We cannot fence God in and say: "Well, if you want to know God, come through this gate." We do not own God; God owns us, and God owns the whole of creation. This is the message of the Bible.

It is this biblical faith that drives us into dialogue. If my Hindu, Buddhist, or Muslim neighbour is as much a child of God as I am, and if nothing that either of us does to reach or know God can fall outside the mercy and the providence of God, then we are indeed brothers and sisters. We are pilgrims, not strangers. We have much to learn from each other. We belong together to God our common creator.

Perhaps this section may be concluded with an interesting insight from a less familiar book in the Bible, which carries a warning against making a private property of God.

The Book of Malachi was written in the fifth century B.C., after the temple of Jerusalem was rebuilt. The prophet's own intention is to call the people of Israel to a renewed faithfulness to God. In fact he is not speaking about God and the people of other faiths. But in the course of challenging the priests to commit themselves to sincere worship, he comes out with a startling statement. "Now, you priests," he says, "try asking God to be good to us. He will not answer your prayer, and it will be your fault... I am not pleased with you, I will not accept the offering you bring to me" (1:9-10).

And then comes the challenge:

> People from one end of the world to the other honour me. Everywhere they burn incense to me and offer acceptable sacrifices. All of them honour me.

It proves nothing. But it stands as a constant reminder that ultimately the point of reference of the biblical religion is the God of creation in whom all people live and to whom all people belong.

2. Two encounters

After these general observations on the Bible and people of other faiths, let us now turn to two specific stories of encounter between persons of different faiths, one from within the Hebrew scriptures and the other from the Christian side.

Let us take first the story of Jonah. Why Jonah? I must confess a personal bias here. Years back, when I was minister of the Methodist Church in Colombo, I decided to give a series of Bible studies on the "minor" prophets. Even though I was familiar with the story of Jonah, it was while preparing for a Bible study on the Book of Jonah that I "saw" the radical nature of its message. My interest in dialogue was kindled, and I came to a new awareness of the theological significance of my neighbours of other faith convictions. For me the Bible has never been the same again!

There is no need to recount the story. It is a familiar story and a Sunday school favourite. Though one must admit that it is remembered more for the whale that swallowed Jonah than for the message it carries!

When Jonah was called by God to go to the great city of Nineveh and speak against it, he decided to set out in the opposite direction in order to get away from that responsibility. Why?

Nineveh was the capital of the great empire of Assyria, Israel's deadly enemy, and one that did not share in its faith. For one reason or another, Jonah did not want to get involved, although at the end of the story he blamed God for all that happened. So instead of going to Nineveh he went to Joppa and got into a ship that was about to sail to Spain.

The rest of the story will be even more readily remembered. The ship is caught in a storm; the sailors discover, by casting lots, the person who has brought upon them the anger of God; Jonah is thrown into the sea; he is brought ashore by the whale that has swallowed him, and is again commissioned by God to go to Nineveh to warn its inhabitants about the impending punishment for the wickedness of the city.

Jonah obeyed this time. The city was so large that it took him three days to walk through it. He gave his message: The Lord has decided to destroy the city for its wickedness. "In forty days Nineveh will be destroyed," he announced (3:4).

Then something that Jonah never expected happened. The people of Nineveh decided that everyone should fast, and all the people, from the greatest to the least, put on clothes of penitence and prayed for forgiveness. Even the king of Nineveh responded to Jonah's message and sent out a proclamation to the people of Nineveh: "This is the order of the King and his officials: no one is to eat anything; all persons, cattle and sheep are forbidden to eat or drink. All persons and all animals must wear sackcloth (the sign of repentance in Semitic culture). Everyone must pray earnestly to God and must give up his wicked behaviour and his evil actions. Perhaps God will change his mind" (3:8).

And the King was right. "God saw what they did... so he changed his mind and did not punish them as he said he would" (3:10).

The most interesting part of the Book of Jonah in fact comes only after this, and it may be helpful to quote the text in full:

> Jonah was very unhappy about this and became angry. So he prayed, "Lord, didn't I say before I left home that this is just what you would do? That's why I did my best to run away to Spain! I knew that you are a loving and merciful God, always patient, always kind, and always ready to change your mind and not punish. Now then, Lord, let me die. I am better off dead than alive."
>
> The Lord answered, "What right do you have to be angry?"
>
> Jonah went out east of the city and sat down. He made a shelter for himself and sat in its shade, waiting to see what would happen to Nineveh. Then the Lord God made a plant grow up over Jonah to give him some shade, so that he would be more comfortable. Jonah was extremely pleased with the plant. But at dawn the next day, at God's command, a worm attacked the plant, and it died. After the sun had risen, God sent a hot east wind, and Jonah was about to faint from the heat of the sun beating down on his head. So he wished he were dead. "I am better off dead than alive," he said.
>
> But God said to him, "What right do you have to be angry about the plant?"
>
> Jonah replied, "I have every right to be angry – angry enough to die!"
>
> The Lord said to him, "This plant grew up in one night and disappeared the next; you didn't do anything for it, and you didn't make it grow – yet you feel sorry for it! How much more, then, should I have pity on Nineveh, that great city. After all, it has more than 120,000 innocent children in it, as well as many animals!"

A careful reader would have already recognized that Jonah is not so much a prophet as a character in the story. The true prophet here is the unknown author of the Book of Jonah who seeks to make a crucial point about God's relationship with humanity. Jonah represents a particular religious perception and understanding of the people of other faiths.

Jonah's annoyance centres around three things. First, he does not expect repentance from the people of Nineveh. For him they are beyond repentance and he does not even call upon them to give up their sinful ways; he simply announces the impending destruction. Secondly, he does not expect God to respond so quickly and so readily, and by so doing to put to shame the prophet of doom God had himself commissioned. Thirdly, Jonah suspects from the beginning that God is not entirely reliable in these matters. That was why he did not want to get involved. He was pressed into service. And then let down. He complains that if God wants to deal with people in his own way, he could at least have left him alone. Now, having predicted the destruction of Nineveh, which God wanted him to do, God has gone back on his word and Jonah himself is discredited. "Now Lord, let me die. I am better off dead than alive."

The Book of Jonah is meant to illustrate God's absolute sovereignty over the whole of creation. It portrays God as God of mercy and love, who would rather forgive than destroy. The point of the Book of Jonah is that this love and mercy of God are not confined to any one nation or people. This "foreign" city and people are as much the concern of God as Jerusalem and Israel; their prayer and repentance are as acceptable to God as anyone else's! God deals with the people of Nineveh with profound compassion.

What, then, does this book tell us about the way we think of and have dealings with people of other faiths?

The second encounter is described in the Acts of the Apostles. In chapter 10 of the book we have the story of the encounter between Peter and a man called Cornelius who is the captain of a Roman regiment. Now Cornelius is a "God-fearer", a name that is given to non-Jews who take an active interest in the teaching of the Torah and hold in honour the God of Israel. He is also active in works of charity.

Cornelius has a vision. He is asked by an angel of God to send for Simon Peter who is at Joppa in the house of another Simon, a leather-worker. He sends three men to invite him to his home in Caesarea.

In the meantime Peter goes up on the roof of the house in order to pray. He has a strange vision.

> He saw the heaven open and something coming down that looked like a large sheet being lowered by its four corners to the earth. In it were all kinds of animals, reptiles, and wild birds. A voice said to him, "Get up, Peter, kill and eat." But Peter said, "Certainly not, Lord! I have never eaten anything ritually unclean or defiled." The voice spoke to him again, "Do not consider anything unclean that God has declared clean." This happened three times and then the thing was taken back up into heaven (Acts 10:11-12).

This vision is the centre of the story, for Cornelius, who had sent his men to bring Peter to him, is a "Gentile". Normally Peter would not enter his house or eat with him. Peter acknowledges this when he enters the house of Cornelius:

> "You yourselves know very well that a Jew is not allowed by his religion to visit or associate with Gentiles. But God has shown me that I must not consider any person ritually unclean or defiled" (v.28).

Then he listens to Cornelius' story of how God approved his prayers and works of charity, and makes his second confession:

> "I now realize that it is true that God treats everyone on the same basis. Whoever worships him and does what is right is acceptable to him; no matter what race he belongs to" (v.34-35).

The whole story is set in the context of the conversion of Cornelius, but in many ways it is also the story of the conversion of Peter. Peter learns, perhaps for the first time, that the religious laws set by religious traditions are not the boundaries within which God operates. Such religious laws are often necessary and they help provide identity, coherence and meaning for particular religious communities. Many of them may have been shaped more by specific cultural and historical necessities than a profound understanding of God and God's relationship with humanity. The real problem begins when these laws are given universal validity and are held as defining the boundaries of God's own activity.

We have had many such instances in the history of the church. At one time there was an attempt to limit the saving activity of God to the confines of the church, insisting that "there is no salvation outside the church". The debate on the relation between conversion and baptism continues to this day. A number of Christians believe that one has to be baptized in order to be saved, and this is being seriously challenged in some parts of the world. It is not our intention here to enter this debate. What is important for us is to recognize that Peter had to undergo a process of conversion in order to meet Cornelius and tell him about Jesus Christ.

But for the vision he had, Peter would have had many problems when the men sent by Cornelius arrived at his door, for he would normally not go to the house of a Gentile, far less eat with him and stay with him. For that encounter to happen, God had to convert Peter to his way of looking at humanity.

Secondly Peter learned the lesson that Jonah also reluctantly learned. That there is no need to "channel" God to people. God has direct access to people, and they stand in a relationship to God.

Christians have always been slow and reluctant to learn this truth. Faced with the undeniable faith and the complete dependence on God in the life of a Muslim, or the deep devotion to God in the prayer of a Hindu, or the compassion and the dedication of a Buddhist, Christians experience a certain reservation to affirm these. Somehow the average Christian would like to feel that all this is not really like Christian faith, Christian devotion and Christian dedication. They are sometimes interpreted as belonging to what is called "natural" revelation which is "not quite the thing". At one time Christian theologians claimed that all these were sociologically interesting but had no transcendental dimension to them.

But in the story of Cornelius we are told that God had heard his prayer and was pleased with his works of charity. It is true that he becomes a disciple of Christ. But long before he ever heard the message, he had stood in a special relationship with God. It was Peter who had to learn that truth. It had never occurred to Peter that God would communicate so directly with someone outside the Jewish religion and not ritually acceptable to his religious tradition. "I now realize", says Peter, "that it is true that God treats everyone on the same basis!"

At the Sixth Assembly of the World Council of Churches in Vancouver, worship played a very important role. There was a children's camp which was run parallel to the Assembly. Its purpose was to expose the Assembly to the children and to bring the concerns of the child to the Assembly. The Worship Committee gave one of the main morning worship services of the Assembly to the children and asked them to plan it. The children wrote their own prayers and songs. The song that captured the imagination of many of the participants of the Assembly was this one:

Black and white and red and yellow
God loves us everyone;
black and white and red and yellow,
God loves us all.
God has no favourite people,
all are alike to him;
God is love, God gives peace,
God loves us all.

It was refreshing to hear from the lips of children the message that Jonah and Peter had to learn with so much pain and trouble!

3. Jesus the only way?

"What about Christ?" somebody is sure to ask. "We do share a common humanity in creation. But didn't God become incarnate in Jesus? Is not Jesus Christ therefore the fullest revelation of God and the saviour of all peoples?"

In fact this view which holds creation as general revelation and Christ as the special or unique revelation is already projected in the scripture. "In the past", says the author of the Letter to the Hebrews, "God spoke to our ancestors many times and in many ways through the prophets, but in these last days he has spoken to us through his Son" (Heb.1:1).

St Paul elaborates on this idea in the opening chapters of his Letter to the Romans. Those who walk in evil will be punished by God, argues Paul, because they already know what is right. "Ever since God created the world, his invisible qualities, both his eternal power and his divine nature, have been clearly seen; they are perceived in the things that God has made. So those people have no excuse at all!" (Rom. 1:20). He goes even further to say that conscience, in the case of the Gentiles, and Law in the case of the Jews, made it possible for people to do what is right. "The Gentiles do not have the Law; but whenever they do by instinct what the Law commands, they are their own law, even though they do not have the Law. Their conduct shows that what the Law commands is written in their hearts. Their consciences also show that this is true since their thoughts sometimes accuse them and sometimes defend them" (Rom. 2:14-15). "But now", Paul continues in chapter 3, "God's way of putting people right through their faith has been revealed... God puts people right through their faith in Jesus Christ" (Rom. 3:21-22).

The rest of the Letter to the Romans, and indeed all the letters of Paul, are an attempt to show that God has acted in a decisively saving way in Jesus the Christ, and that one can enter this salvation through faith in him.

"If this is the burden of the Christian scriptures, what is the purpose of dialogue? Our task is only one of proclamation, in which we present Jesus the Christ as the saviour of the world" – many Christians would claim.

Such an understanding is further strengthened by what are generally called the "exclusive verses" in the Bible which present Christ as unique, and the only way to God and salvation.

For the sake of convenience, let us gather together some of the so-called exclusive sayings, before we take a second look at them on the basis of the total teaching presented in the Christian scriptures. Some of these verses have to do with the person of Jesus. For example:

> For God so loved the world that he gave his only begotten Son, so that everyone that believes in him may not die but have eternal life... whoever believes in the Son is not judged; but whoever does not believe has already been judged, because he has not believed in God's only Son (John 3:16,18).
>
> Thomas said to him, "Lord, we do not know where you are going; so how can we know the way to get there?" Jesus answered him, "I am the way, the truth, and the life; no one goes to the Father except by me" (John 14:5-6).

Some other statements concern the intention of God, and the best illustration is in the Book of Acts. Peter and John are taken to the High Priest, following the healing of a man born lame, and Peter bears a bold witness to Christ:

> Jesus is the one of whom the scripture says, "The stone that you builders despised turned out to be the most important of all." Salvation is to be found through him alone; in all the world there is no one else whom God has given who can save us (Acts 4:11-12).

Finally there are exclusive statements on the nature of the salvation that Jesus is said to have brought.

The Letter to the Hebrews argues that Christ's is the last and final sacrifice:

> So God does away with all the old sacrifices and puts the sacrifice of Christ in their place. Because Jesus Christ did what God wanted him to do, we all are purified from sin by the offering that he made in his own body once and for all (Heb. 10:9-10).

Jesus is the one mediator of all humanity, says Paul:

> ...This is good and it pleases God our Saviour, who wants everyone to be saved and to come to know the truth. For there is one God, and there is one who brings God and mankind together, the man Christ Jesus, who gave himself to redeem all mankind (1 Tim. 2:3-6).

What can we say about these claims to uniqueness that are clearly set forth in such scriptural verses? Can there be any case for dialogue in view of these unequivocal assertions about the decisiveness and finality of what God has done in Christ?

Before we look at these sayings and their meaning, we should turn to the rest of the scripture and see how it relates to them. For it is dangerous to develop a whole theology or missiology on the basis of a few verses. Since most of these texts refer to Jesus, it would be good to turn to Jesus himself and to his teaching as presented in other parts of the scripture.

When we consider the Synoptic Gospels, i.e. Matthew, Mark and Luke, we see a Jesus who is somewhat different from the Jesus presented by John. This does not of course mean that the Synoptic Gospels are free of interpretation. Scholars have shown that each of the Gospel writers has a particular purpose in the way he selects, arranges and introduces the stories and teachings of Jesus. It is generally agreed, however, that St John's Gospel takes far more freedom with the material related to Jesus than the others. John, more than the others, shapes the material about Jesus, including what he is said to have taught, in ways that reflect the faith of the early church about the person of Jesus.

The most striking fact in the Synoptics is Jesus' own God-centred life. He never calls himself the Son of God, but the son of man. Even more important, Jesus sees his primary function as the initiator of the kingdom of God (Mark 1:14-15; Luke 11:20). He announces the forgiveness that accompanies the coming of the kingdom, calls persons to repentance and challenges them to a profoundly ethical understanding of the relationship between God and the human person and between human persons. It is God who offers life to all who enter the kingdom. Jesus' own life is entirely God-centred, God-dependent and God-ward. In the Synoptic environment it would be strange if Jesus were to say "I and the father are one," or "I am the way, the truth and the life." There seems to be no claim to divinity or to oneness with God; what we have is the challenge to live lives that are totally turned towards God.

It is also of interest that Jesus claims that he has come not to abolish the Law, a claim that Paul and the writer of the Hebrews make later. When challenged that he was breaking the law, Jesus claimed that he was in fact fulfilling the law in its true intention. He gives the summary of the law as the summary of his own teachings (Deut. 6:4; Lev. 19:18; Mark 12:28-34).

While Jesus does urge people to "follow" him, to become his "disciples", to believe in him and what he teaches, he never seems to suggest that he is the mediator, much less the only mediator, between God and the human person. He seems to identify himself more with the suffering servant of Isaiah.

We see primarily a teacher, one who tells stories, speaks in parables, mixes with the despised people. We see one who loves and enjoys ordinary people, the masses.

Jesus also seems to place enormous emphasis on the actual life lived and the actual attitudes held, so much more indeed than on what is said or believed. A radical move away from the self towards a God-centred life (life in the kingdom) seems to be the main burden of his teaching. He does not ask people to leave their religious community and follow him. He has a small group of people who are with him most of the time. He has called them to him and asked them to be with him. But he shows no anxiety that everyone should become his immediate follower (Mark 10:38-41).

We need not labour this point. All we want to show is that there is another witness to Jesus, different from the one that emerges when all the exclusive sayings are put together, and this witness in some ways stands in contradiction to the Jesus presented in those sayings. It is clear that St John makes use of most of the incidents in the life of Jesus to introduce theological discourses on the significance of Jesus to the faith community of his time.

The distinction between the Synoptic Gospels and the Gospel of John should not be overstated. Quite a few scholars claim that all accounts, including the Synoptic accounts, are accounts of faith, moulded by the experience of the early church. Some would even claim that we can never know exactly who Jesus was in actual history and what he really taught. Everything has gone through the "factory of faith" and what we have in the Gospel accounts represents what people thought Jesus was, or what they wanted us to believe of him. But most scholars are convinced that the authors of the Synoptic Gospels, although inevitably influenced by their own faith perspective, give us a reasonably reliable account of who Jesus was and what he taught. Of course there are those who see no reason why the witness of St John cannot be as valid as the Synoptics. We need not enter this controversy. We need only to keep in mind the difference in perspective and presentation.

What is important to realize, in short, is that there is a "Christ of faith" to whom there is a clear witness in the New Testament. St Paul and the author of the Letter to the Hebrews, for example, show little or no interest in Jesus' teachings or indeed in his ministry among his own people. They are primarily interested in the "meaning" of Jesus' death and resurrection, and see no reason why they should not bear testimony to it. It was only natural that the community of faith reflected on the meaning of the Christ-event for their own lives. John appears to be half-way between the Synoptics and Paul in his attempt to bring out this meaning through interpreting the events in the life of Jesus and his teachings. This he does in the light of his own beliefs about Jesus.

What does this amount to? Does it mean that John, Paul and the author of the Letter to the Hebrews are not reliable guides to our understanding of who Jesus was? Does this mean that we must discount their testimony that Jesus is the Son of God, the Christ, the mediator, the way, the truth and the life? By no means. John, Paul, Peter and others are all part of the Christian tradition; they tell us what Jesus meant to his immediate followers and to the early church. Their witness is an essential part of the Christian heritage about Jesus and his significance.

What we should remember, however, is that these are all statements of faith about Jesus the Christ. They derive their meaning in the context of faith, and have no meaning outside the community of faith. They hold enormous significance for Christian people, today as much as in the past. They were absolutely valid for those who confessed Christ in centuries gone by, and they continue to be valid for those of us who belong to that tradition of confession.

But we should not assume that these confessions were definitive. The scriptures witness to the struggle that the community of faith had to go through in order to understand the significance of Jesus. Many different titles were used for Jesus; many terms, like salvation, reconciliation, new creation, etc., were used to describe what God had done for them in Christ. John even went to the Jewish Wisdom tradition, and made use of the concept of the eternal word in his attempt to understand and interpret the meaning of the Christ-event.

This, then, is the right setting in which to understand the exclusive statements that claim uniqueness for Christ. The claims that the Christ is the only way, the only Saviour, the one Mediator, etc., are made in the language of faith, and should be understood within the context of the church's faith-commitment.

The excessive emphasis on *only* is part of the early Christian polemics against the Jewish people from whom the Christians were growing out as a separate community. That community was a small one. Its faith was strong and secure, on the one hand; it was constantly under attack, on the other. The community was under immense pressure to justify its faith in Jesus, the crucified master whom they now experienced as the risen Lord. As much by the logic of the circumstances as by the strength of their convictions they were led to make claims for Jesus which he would not perhaps have made for himself.

Part of this development is also marked by a significant shift from the theocentric attitude that characterized Jesus' own teaching. Gradually Jesus comes to the centre and God is pushed to the periphery. God is not celebrated as the saviour, but Christ is the saviour. Our new life is rooted not in God but in Christ. In Christian usage even the phrase "through Jesus Christ" in our prayers turns out to be prayer to Christ.

All these developments are of course understandable; and some of them may well have arisen out of the experience of the faith community that the God whom they knew in creation is the same God whom they encountered in Christ and in their experience of the Holy Spirit. The doctrine of the Trinity was developed within the church to provide a framework of understanding to the developing beliefs about Jesus Christ. We should recognize, however, that all these developments are part of the growing faith-perspectives about Jesus and his significance.

It may be pointed out that something not entirely dissimilar happened to another historical person, Gautama Buddha. He was a prince who became an ascetic. Through an experience of enlightenment, he found a way which, he was convinced, was the way by which all human beings might escape the problem of life and enter a state of bliss. He clearly said that there was no need to know him, believe in him or worship him, but that anyone who saw the true nature of life and followed the way (the Middle Path) could attain Buddhahood and *nirvana*.

Gautama's followers, however, saw in him far more than what he claimed for himself. Today in some branches of Buddhism, Buddha is held to be divine. His previous incarnations are described in detail, and as "Lord Buddha" he has become the centre of veneration, indeed of worship.

Many Christians are likely to be offended by such a comparison. They will feel that in making it we are either being cynical or indeed we expose our lack of conviction about Christ.

But it need not be so. The comparison is made because I know many Buddhists for whom the conviction about the divinity of the Lord Buddha is so central that they will give their lives to defend it. For them there is nothing mythical about it, and questions of developments within the tradition have nothing to do with it. For them the Buddha is indeed divine, and anyone who doubts it or fails to recognize it has not come to see the truth. They will never accept this as a later accretion. For them it represents the fuller understanding of who the Buddha actually was. And they will find plenty of support for it in their scriptures.

Can a Christian turn around and say to the Buddhist that he or she is misguided to think this way about the Lord Buddha? We have no grounds to do so. For the Buddhists, from their perspective, will see an almost parallel development in the teachings of the church about Christ, and they will call in question a number of beliefs about Christ. And yet Christians know how meaningful and central their beliefs are to the community of faith.

All this is to say that the exclusive statements about Christ can never be understood unless we recognize the different levels in which language is used, and the different standpoints from which claims are made. Let me illustrate.

When my daughter tells me that I am the best daddy in the world, and there can be no other father like me, she is speaking the truth. For this comes out of her experience. She is honest about it; she knows no other person in the role of her father. The affirmation is part and parcel of her being. There are no doubts about it in her mind. She may be totally disillusioned if she is told that in fact her father is not the best daddy in the world.

But of course it is not true in another sense. For one thing, I myself know friends who, I think, are better fathers than I am. Even more importantly, one should be aware that in the next house there is another little girl who also thinks that her daddy is the best father in the whole world. And she too is right. In fact at the level of the way the two children relate to their fathers, no one from outside can compare the two fathers and say which one of them is a better father. It is impossible to compare the truth content of the statements of the two girls. For here we are dealing not with absolute truths, but with the language of faith and love.

This does not of course mean that there are no objective ways of finding out whether a person is fulfilling the role of father in a faithful way. We cannot assert that there are no objective criteria to distinguish a good father from a bad one, and that there is only subjective experience on which to rely.

But that will make no difference to the child's claim about the father and the exclusive language in which that claim will be expressed. Within the child's experience, and in the child's world, the claim will be an absolute one.

The language of the Bible is also the language of faith. Whether we are speaking about the chosen people, or about Jesus as the only way, we are expressing a relationship that has profound meaning and significance for us. We do not say it lightly, for such belief is at the heart of our whole experience. But we should never claim that such beliefs are formulated or held to discredit other beliefs. They express our own convictions, even as other beliefs express the convictions others have.

The problem begins when we take these confessions in the language of faith and love and turn them into absolute truths. It becomes much more serious when we turn them into truths on the basis of which we begin to measure the truth or otherwise of other faith-claims. My daughter cannot say to her little friend in the next house that there is no way that she can have the best father, for the best one is right there in her house. If she does, we will have to dismiss it as child-talk!

In some theological circles this way of understanding the Christian claims about Christ will be frowned upon and looked at with great suspicion. This, they will claim, relativizes the faith. Still others will say that if the absolute claims for Christ are not objective truths, but only the claims of faith, then we have nothing to hold on to. Christianity will then be reduced to a purely subjective experience. They will say that what we believe in should be true independent of our belief or experience. In their view the claims to uniqueness for Christ must be a matter of *fact* and not merely a confession of *faith*.

One can understand such anxiety, but the view takes little account of actual human limitations on the one hand and the nature of absolute truth on the other. Truth in the absolute sense is beyond anyone's grasp, and we should not say that the Christian claims about Jesus are absolute because St John, St Paul and the scriptures make them. There will be others who make similar claims based on authorities they set for themselves. Such claims to absolute truth lead only to intolerance and arrogance and to unwarranted condemnation of each others' faith-perspectives.

On the other hand, there is no reason why one should not make a full and sincere commitment based on a faith-claim or a truth-claim based on faith. That is the essence of having "faith"; it is based not on certain knowledge but on the certainty of faith itself.

The insistence on absolute and objective truth comes from certain cultural and philosophical traditions that are alien to the Bible. For what we have in the Bible are not attempts to project objective truths, but a struggle to understand, to celebrate, to witness and to relate. There are in the Bible many traditions, many movements, many pictures, many confessions and many claims. Sometimes they are complementary; at other times they are at variance with each other. But what emerges is a story of genuine faith and the celebration of that faith in convinced witness.

Such an understanding of the biblical witness, and especially of those exclusive verses which have often been treated as absolute truths and used to deny the faiths of others, will free us as faithful people to be in dialogue with other faithful people. For truth, when understood this way, can only be shared. There is nothing to defend, nothing to thrust upon others, nothing to "sell". It may well be that persons of other faiths are likely to be impressed more by those who, in humility, are prepared to share their spiritual struggles and their witness of faith than by those who claim to have objective truth beyond debate and dispute.

There are those who would claim that the Christian claims to absolute truth are not based on the power of the human person to *know*, but on the revelation given by God. But this solves nothing. For most religions, like Islam and Hinduism, are also based on the concept of revelation; and throughout history different persons have claimed to have various revelations from God. Revelation itself is part of the faith-claim, and its validity also has to do with the faith of the community.

It is therefore very important that Christians recognize the nature of biblical faith and its language, and relate to others, in the conviction that others too have a witness to offer. Exclusive claims, presented as absolute truths, only result in alienation. They are not the proverbial "stone of stumbling" but obstacles that are placed in the way of people, which prevent them from knowing Jesus whose life was marked by self-giving.

In fact Christians are called in the Bible not to make claims, but to make a commitment that opens their lives to others. And others also have their commitments. Dialogue thus is an encounter of commitments. It is in this encounter that people are able to see and hear the witness we have to offer to one another.

4. A biblical basis for dialogue?

In the monthly *Letter on Evangelism* (August 1982), one of the readers from India recalled the following incident:

> Once a Gandhian leader came to Kohima and we had fellowship with him. As I was sitting by him, he started conversing with me about religious matters: "There are some extreme Christians who say that man can be saved through Christ only and there is no other way. What is your view?" "It is what I believe," I replied. "There are millions and millions of people in other major religions of the world. What will be their fate?" he hastily asked. "According to the Bible those who do not believe in Christ will perish," I replied. He angrily departed.
>
> My conviction is that whether we like it or not we cannot compromise the truth.

This is a revealing story. First it shows how, in a country like India, no one really needs to organize dialogues between persons of different faiths. Sitting beside the others on a social occasion provides the opportunity for what can be a fascinating Hindu-Christian dialogue.

Secondly, note that the Hindu partner left the scene deeply hurt, not because he lost the argument, but because there was no conversation at all! For a Hindu the Christian attitude would have appeared as an extreme form of intolerance.

Of course there are many Christians who are convinced that Christ is the "only way", but they will not close the conversation. They will have dialogue with the Gandhian leader, and perhaps even make it an occasion for Christian witness.

Yet the story is not untypical. It illustrates the attitude of millions of Christians in Asia and elsewhere towards people of other faiths. The Christian partner in the story displays a certain intolerance which seems almost against his own nature: "Whether we like it or not," he says, "we cannot compromise the truth". And what is this truth? "According to the Bible, those who do not believe in Christ will perish"! He does not want them to, but as a Christian he must accept the Bible's verdict.

There is a fundamental issue at stake here. Is the Bible against a dialogical relationship with neighbours of other faiths? Or is the biblical message, however carefully, courteously and humbly it is presented, uncompromising in its demand that every one must believe in and accept Jesus Christ in order to be saved?

There is little hope, in such an understanding, for people of other faiths.

In order to show that the attitude reflected in the story is not part of "popular" belief, but is based on certain clear theological convictions and a certain interpretation of the Bible, let me quote from a recent book:

> We cannot be neutral observers of other religions. In the first place the Gospel of Jesus Christ comes to us with a built-in prejudgment of all other faiths so that we know in advance of our study what we must ultimately conclude about them. They give meaning to life apart from that which God has given in the biblical story culminating in Jesus Christ, and they organize life outside the covenant community of Jesus Christ. Therefore, devoid of this saving knowledge and power of God, these faiths not only are unable to bring men to God, they actually lead men away from God and hold them captive from God. This definitive and blanket judgment... is not derived from our investigation of the religions, but is given in the structure and content of Gospel faith itself.[1]

Let us for the moment not deal with this attitude of making "definitive and blanket judgments" without even studying other faiths. For, the most serious statement here is that such an evaluation is to be found in the "structure and content of the Gospel faith itself".

Is this really so? Is the biblical message so negative about those who do not accept and believe in Jesus, the Christ? Or is there another way to understand and read the Gospels that could become a different basis for our relationship with those who do not believe the way we do?

God's dialogue with the world

Few people will dispute that the heart of the Bible is the affirmation of God's loving relationship with human beings. There is in the Bible the affirmation that God is love. As a statement about the nature of ultimate reality, or as a description of what God is like, such a statement may evoke little controversy. The Bible, however, does not stop with the affirmation that God is love. In fact the Gospels tell the story of what it *means* to be loving. That is the Good News. The gospel reveals

---

[1] Edmund Perry, *The Gospel in Dispute*, Garden City, N.Y. Doubleday & Co., 1958, p.83.

the nature of God's love; it reveals what it actually meant for God in terms of God's relationship with the world.

The affirmation that God was in Christ, therefore, has a very special meaning. It is a claim that in the life and ministry of Jesus we come to know about God and God's relationship with human beings. We are not dealing with the Christological question of how or in what sense God was in Christ. All that we can say from the witness of those who lived with Christ and experienced Christ is that they were convinced that, meeting him, they came into a living encounter with God. It is in this sense that Bishop J.A.T. Robinson speaks about Jesus becoming a "window" into God. Those who believe that in Jesus they had a "glimpse" into the nature of God should ask themselves as to what indeed they were able to "see" of God in Jesus' life. When the question is put in this way, dialogue is seen to be at the heart of the gospel.

For the gospel is not a message of rejection; it is a message of acceptance. Jesus preached a message of acceptance and claimed that God already accepts people even before they turn to him. Repentance, in Jesus' teaching, is not a condition for acceptance, it is a response to the acceptance that God has already extended to all persons. The problem that Jesus had with some of his contemporaries was that he extended this acceptance, in practice, to all kinds of people who in popular view were not "acceptable".

Jesus also rooted this message in his understanding of the nature of God. In love God relates to people; there is no other way God can relate to people, for love is of the essence of God. God "makes his sun to shine on bad and good people alike, and gives rain to those who do good and to those who do evil" (Matt. 5:45).

To say, therefore, that God will not love you unless you repent, or that God will not save you unless you believe in what God has done in Jesus Christ, is to reverse the order of the gospel message. It seriously distorts the gospel and presents a message that is alien to the biblical understanding of God.

God's love is unconditional. It is because God loves us that the gospel calls us to repent – to turn around from a life centred on the self – and begin a life centred on God's love and acceptance.

Jesus' attitude to children illustrates this aspect of the gospel message. The disciples were trying to prevent the parents from bringing the children to Jesus (Mark 10:13-16). We do not know why exactly they stood between Jesus and the children. It could be that the child, the disciples felt, would not be able to understand or respond to the teachings of Jesus. Why waste the Master's time on children when he should be teaching the adults and calling them to the discipleship of the kingdom! Or it could simply be that they considered children to be a nuisance, as many people do.

But Jesus insists on receiving them. He goes further. He says that the kingdom of God belongs to them. On another occasion he goes to the extent of declaring that unless one becomes like a child one cannot enter the kingdom of God.

Here the biblical message is unambiguously dialogical. For it insists on the "previousness" of grace, and of God's acceptance of us before our acceptance of God. The people we meet, of whatever religion, race or age, are all in that sense people of God. It is this belief that the other person is as much a child of God as I am that should form the basis of our relationship with our neighbours. That attitude is at the heart of being in dialogue.

Dialogue is also at the very heart of the cross. Jesus' death is understood and interpreted in many ways. But, among other things, the cross surely stands for the vulnerability of love. Jesus, in his passion and death, acts out the consequences of his teaching on love. To the end he refused to hate and to reject. With those who dealt unjustly with him, he was invariably patient. True to his own message he never failed people. He would rather be rejected than reject. What marked his life and his message was total availability. In that sense the incarnation is God's dialogue with the world. It is an expression of how God always stands with the human community.

That is to say, interfaith dialogue is based on acceptance, which is at the heart of the gospel message, an acceptance that is not demanding, but self-giving. It is the ability to accept the other in his or her otherness. If we cannot accept others as God's children until they believe as we do, then we do not act or speak from within the message of the gospel. If we say that those who do not believe in Christ and do not belong to the Christian community are outside the saving providence and power of

God, we are talking about a God who is not the God of Jesus Christ. For the distinctive message that Jesus gave, which in fact made his news *good* news, is that God loves us first and that his love is unchanging and unfailingly available.

The belief that people of other faiths are outside the saving activity of God is not only a comment about the people, but also about God. The God of the Bible, the God whom Jesus called Father, rules over all and is in all. All things have their being in God.

In other words, I want to claim that the central message of the Bible is deeply dialogical. It is unfortunate that much of our attitude towards other faiths developed mainly out of our reading of the exclusive verses of the Bible, not out of its central message. We are in dialogue precisely because our God is the God whom Jesus revealed to us, and we believe in the profound love of God that embraces all humanity. God is our freedom, setting us free and making us open so that we can meet and talk with our neighbours of other faiths, treating them as our brothers and sisters. We do not reject our neighbours or condemn them simply because acceptance and understanding are the corner-stone of the gospel message.

Jesus' attitude to false religion

"All this is true, but it is only part of the truth," it could be objected, "for there is in the life and teachings of Jesus a clear rejection of certain aspects of religion and a call to repentance and commitment to a new way of life." Isn't there indeed an implied rejection of all religions in the gospel?

Implicit in such a view is a sharp distinction between people and their religion. It would claim that while God loves people, the gospel rejects all religions. It is people whom God redeems and not religious systems, which are "pagan" and work against God. This attitude is described – and criticized by the editors themselves – in a dramatic way in a recent book:

> ... approach to other religions has been to view them as systems which are pagan, heathen, and closed to the activity of God in history. They are anti-Christian systems which have no signs of redemption in them. Only the people in them are redeemable. The system itself is not redeemable. Therefore the approach is to confront the systems by hurling gospel grenades

34

over the boundary walls in a process designed to raze the religious system to the ground. While this siege is in progress, the attacking forces rescue what inmates they can, clean them up, baptize them, and then use them as frontline troops in the siege operations.[2]

Implicit in the view described above is a serious misunderstanding, that other religions, like a large part of Protestant Christianity, have to do with cerebral beliefs and systems of thought which can be separated from the persons who hold those beliefs. What is even stranger is the simple assumption that all religions are against God. Further, here is an attempt to separate religion from history, which can be called in question. Often life, religion and history are inseparable. In those situations what does it mean to proclaim God as the Lord of life or of history?

But let us return to the Bible and ask the question whether Jesus was against the religion of his time. Did he draw a sharp distinction between the gospel and the prevalent religion, and reject the religion of the people in favour of the gospel?

There is no doubt that Jesus rejected hypocrisy, self-righteousness, the kind of religion that was outward and ceremonial and devoid of spiritual meaning. But there is little or no evidence that he rejected the religion of the people, or condemned it. He himself regularly worshipped in the synagogue; he was familiar with the Torah, visited the Temple and kept the feasts. He claimed that he came to fulfill the Law and not to abolish it. Nowhere is the suggestion that people should reject Judaism and relinquish religion altogether.

For Jesus, false religion is that which substitutes external ceremony for internal spirituality. The whole of the Sermon on the Mount is a call to "internalize" the law so that it becomes a spiritual spring-board for authentic action based on love.

Of course Jesus announced the in-breaking of the kingdom of God; he did call people to a radical repentance, away from the self and turned towards God; he did teach that religion is more a matter of relationships than of belief systems and ceremonies.

[2] *Sharing Jesus in the Two Thirds World*, ed. Vinay Samuel and Chris Sugden. Grand Rapids, Eerdmans, 1983, p.132.

But none of these took the form of anti-religious "grenade-throwing exercise".

The Christian rejection of Hinduism, Buddhism and Islam is therefore not to be equated with Jesus' challenge to the religious tradition of his time. Jesus was part of that religion. He, like many of the prophets before him, was challenging his own tradition to become true to its calling. That was why he was seen as a teacher and prophet by his own people.

Of course we do not know what Jesus would have said if he were to comment on "other" religious traditions! The few instances where the Gospels record Jesus' encounter with outsiders to Judaism do not really help us to come to any conclusions. But there were cases when Jesus was surprised to find that the so-called "outsiders", like the Canaanite woman, were more responsive to his teaching than some among his own people (Matt. 15:21-28).

Jesus was in dialogue with his own religious tradition. He affirmed it, but he also challenged it where it seemed to stray from its true purpose and intentions. He had new perceptions of what God intends for human lives, he gave expression to them within an overall attitude of participation and involvement in his own religious tradition.

That is why it is difficult to accept the position that other religious traditions are outside "the saving knowledge and power of God". It is even more difficult to accept it when the judgment is made without listening to, learning from, understanding and participating in those religious traditions and when the rejection is claimed to result from the "structure and content of the gospel message itself".

How can we make such assertions if we do believe that love, self-giving and vulnerability are at the heart of the gospel message? One must admit that Christians of some of the dominant cultures have heavily overplayed the "judging" aspect of the gospel message. Instead of seeing the gospel as judging and challenging their own lives and religious values, they have used it to condemn, and even to reject other religious traditions and their adherents. It is now important to recover the attitude of dialogue as an essential component of our relationship with other people and their faiths. Because that attitude is consistent with the teaching and the witness of the Jesus whom we meet in the scriptures.

Discerning the kingdom

Dialogue also has to do with discernment, and the call to discernment is central to the message of Jesus. His life and his teaching pointed to the reign of God. As we said elsewhere, this reign or kingdom of God is under no one's control. It is invisible and mysterious; no one knows its limits or its extent. It is not easy to discern where it is and where it is not.

But the truly radical nature of the kingdom lies in the fact that it has little to do with religious boundaries. The reign of God breaks into human life, and not into the life of one community or another. If we truly believe that God's kingdom is at work in the whole of human history then we will need to discern it in all kinds of lives and in all sorts of places. The parable of the sheep and the goats is a constant reminder of such participation in the reign of God by those who have little or no consciousness of it (Matt. 25:31-46).

The belief in the kingdom urges us to dialogue. For surely it cannot be that there is only one witness to a kingly rule that embraces all life and all of life; surely there are no situations and persons that God cannot use to further the cause of the kingdom. And how can we discern if we are not even prepared to listen to and learn from what God is doing in other lives. Dialogue can become the engagement in which Christians discern and celebrate the truly universal sweep of the rule of God over all life.

Scriptural witness to the universality of Christ

The truly universal nature of God's rule is a theme on which the Bible dwells at many points. We have already seen how the Old Testament prophets constantly struggled to understand God's relationship with Israel within the context of God's relationship with and rule over all nations. The theme is persistent in the Psalms. The eschatological hope, whether it is in Isaiah or in the Book of Revelation, has to do with the whole of the universe, and not with parts or segments of it.

The New Testamant writers understood the significance of Jesus in its truly universal dimension. Paul is in constant dialogue with his own Jewish tradition, not to deny the reality of the faith of Abraham, Isaac and Jacob, but to link it to Christ and what Christ means. John seeks to do this by speaking of Jesus as the incarnation of the pre-existent Word, who was in the beginning, and through whom all things were made. The Word is described as the light that lightens everyone that comes into the world.

There is no doubt that the scriptures see the Christ-event as having a universal significance. But what does it mean for the way we look at the world, and especially for our dealings with people who live by other faith convictions? Some tend to divide the world into two camps – those who believe in Jesus Christ and thereby receive salvation; and those who have either refused to believe or have not had the opportunity to believe and thus do not participate in this salvation. In this view the only way to be right with God is to repent and believe in Jesus Christ. There is a good example of this position in the Lausanne Covenant. Speaking of the uniqueness and universality of Christ it says:

> We affirm that there is only one Saviour and only one Gospel, although there is a wide diversity of evangelistic approaches. We recognize that all men have some knowledge of God through his general revelation in nature. But we deny that this can save, for men suppress the truth by their unrighteousness. We also reject as derogatory to Christ and the gospel every kind of syncretism and dialogue which implies that Christ speaks equally through all religions and ideologies. Jesus Christ, being himself the only Godman, who gave himself as the only ransom for sinners, is the only mediator between God and man. There is no other name by which we must be saved. All men are perishing because of sin, but God loves all men, not wishing that any should perish but that all should repent. Yet those who reject Christ repudiate the joy of salvation and condemn themselves to eternal separation from God. To proclaim Jesus as "the Saviour of the World" is not to affirm that all men are either automatically or ultimately saved, still less to affirm that all religions offer salvation in Christ. Rather it is to proclaim God's love for a world of sinners and to invite all men to respond to him as Saviour and Lord in the whole-hearted personal commitment of repentance and faith. Jesus Christ has been exalted above every other name; we long for the day when every knee shall bow to him and every tongue shall confess him Lord.

Here the biblical understanding of the universality of Christ is given one particular interpretation. Yes, Christ is universal insofar as the salvation offered in him is available to all persons. But all persons should hear the message, repent, and believe in him in order to be saved.

The word "only" is used again and again. Only one Saviour, only one Gospel, only Godman, only ransom, only mediator. The emphasis is on the assertion that there is no other name by which one should be saved. Here indeed is an exclusivistic way of interpreting the biblical understanding of universality.

The late D.T. Niles was of the opinion that this way of interpreting the universality of Christ goes against the doctrine of grace: "The issue of salvation or otherwise of humankind cannot be stated in terms of human beings' belief or disbelief in the salvation offered in Christ. It has to do with what Christ does with the human family." Without entering into this particular debate I wish only to show that there are other implications of the universality of Christ.

It is indeed possible to understand the significance of the biblical witness to the universality of Jesus Christ in a way that places Christ, and not the human being, at the centre. Viewed thus, dialogue becomes the most natural way to relate to the rest of humanity precisely because Christ is universal! This is how Metropolitan Paulos Mar Gregorios, for example, understands the biblical teaching on the universality of Christ:

> Christ is the first-born of creation, the head of all created reality. He loves not only all men and women, but also all that is created. I am united to Christ in baptism and confirmation. My mind is the mind of Christ. Therefore my love is non-exclusive and open to the whole creation. Nothing is alien or threatening. Love and compassion for the whole creation is the characteristic of Christ. The church as his body shares in this love and compassion. I as a member of that body have to express that love and compassion in faithfulness, integrity and openness, with sympathetic understanding. This is sufficient and compelling reason for me to engage in dialogue with people of other faiths. It is love in Christ that sends me to dialogue.

These two statements come from two very different church traditions. They both affirm the universality of Christ, but one of them is uncompromising and exclusive, and leaves no room for genuine dialogue. In the other the very affirmation of the universality of Christ becomes the basis for a dialogue relationship with people of all religious persuasions.

5. Witness and dialogue

> The whole concept of 'mutual witness' is an invention of the Dialogue department! It is non-biblical and has nothing to do with the way the New Testament understands Christian witness. In the Acts of the Apostles, for instance, it is the Christians who had something to witness to; there we read the story of the proclamation of the gospel and the invitation to respond to it.

That was said by a participant at a WCC meeting. The occasion was the official approval of the text of the "Ecumenical Considerations on Jewish-Christian Dialogue" for study and use in the churches.

The view is by no means uncommon. There are many, even among those who understand and affirm the practice of dialogue, who feel the same way. Once we leave the world of Jesus' dealing with people, we are faced with the story of the early church, as it interprets the significance of Jesus (as in St John's Gospel, for example) and as it goes about its mission (as in the Acts of the Apostles). In both, they claim, we have a non-dialogical stance.

It is important, therefore, in a consideration of the Bible and the people of living faiths, that we take a close look at this part of the Bible.

We must begin with the affirmation that dialogue does not exclude witness. In fact, where people have no convictions to share, there can be no real dialogue. In a multilateral dialogue meeting in Colombo, one of the Hindu participants rejected any idea of "levelling down" religious convictions, and said that he had no interest in entering into dialogue with Christians who had no convictions about their faith. In any genuine dialogue authentic witness must take place, for partners will bear testimony to why they have this or that conviction.

Our discussion, therefore, is not about the appropriateness or the legitimacy of bearing witness; it is about the assumptions one makes about other faiths in witness situations, and the spirit and intention with which the witness is given.

A good deal of Christian witness has been modelled on the Acts of the Apostles. The church's mission down the ages has drawn much inspiration from the preaching in the Acts and from the missionary journeys of St Paul. The present missionary activity is seen in some sense as the continuation of the "world outreach" that began with the "acts" of the apostles. The kind of "straight proclamation of the gospel" that we have in the Acts is often seen as a model for relating to Buddhists, Hindus, Muslims, and others. The dialogue enterprise appears to undercut this basically biblical way in which mission is carried out. Can the Acts of the Apostles serve as a model for my relationship with Hindus, Buddhists and Muslims?

To answer that question, we must look at the context in which the mission described in the Acts took place. That is a specific context which cannot be reproduced. When we take the Acts as a model, without reference to the situation in which the acts took place, we do less than justice to the book.

There are some who see the whole of Acts not so much as a record of the actual preaching and ministry of Peter, Paul and others as Luke's account of the expansion of the church in the early years. We do not wish to enter this particular biblical debate; we shall only look at the sermons and teachings as Luke records them.

Most of the characters who appear in the Acts are Jews or people who were familiar with the Jewish tradition and religion. The apostles were all Jews, and they were all directly or indirectly related to Jesus himself and to his ministry among his people.

Much of the preaching in the Acts is centred on the internal debate within the Jewish community on who Jesus was. The most outstanding question of course was whether Jesus was the long-expected Messiah (Christ) who would deliver the people from their bondage.

The controversy had surfaced even during the time of Jesus. Some of the people recognized him as a rabbi, others as a prophet, and still others as the "one sent by God to save his people". There were different conceptions among them of what the Messiah would do in the process of liberating the people. Some saw him as a political hero who would deliver them from the bondage of Rome, while others expected him to usher in the messianic age that would bring about lasting *shalom* and the immediate presence of God. To many others the political and the eschatological were two aspects of the same concept.

Jesus' ministry was so successful that it threatened to become a mass movement. His entry into Jerusalem, often described as "triumphal", though it was a symbol of humility, to take one example, was seen as a threat both to the religious and political institutions of the land. Finally the authorities from both sides got together to put an end to the movement by sending Jesus to the cross. With the death of Jesus, the whole movement appeared to have collapsed.

The direct experience of the risen Christ, therefore, had a tremendous impact upon the disciples. Now they were convinced that Jesus, whom the authorities rejected and crucified, was the Messiah foretold by the prophets.

We should recognize that at this stage there were no "Christians" in the strict sense of the word; there were only Jewish followers of the Jewish prophet Jesus, whom the authorities denounced and, as they thought, had liquidated. The followers of Jesus worshipped in the temple and kept the Mosaic law, but they had a story to tell their people.

The early apostolic preaching, therefore, must be seen within this controversy over who Jesus was. The first sermon preached by Peter and recorded in Acts 2 is a good illustration:

> Listen to these words, fellow Israelites! Jesus of Nazareth was a man whose divine authority was clearly proven to you by all the miracles and wonders which God performed through him. You yourselves know this, for it happened here among you. In accordance with his own plan, God had already decided that Jesus would be handed over to you; and you killed him by letting sinful men crucify him. But God raised him from death, setting him free from its power, because it was impossible that death should hold him prisoner.... All the people of Israel, then, are to know for sure that this Jesus, whom you crucified, is the one that God has made Lord and Messiah! (2:22-24,36).

Peter is speaking to "fellow Israelites". He claims that the resurrection is the proof that Jesus is indeed the Messiah. In the parts not quoted here, Peter cites Jewish scriptures to authenticate the claim.

The preaching of course led to a division; people took sides on the question. Eventually it resulted in a more distinct community within the Jewish community, which now bore the name of Christ. The prevalent sign for repentance, baptism, was adopted by the members of this community, which later, when administered in the name of Jesus, was also to become the mark of belonging to this community.

But the main point to note here is that, since Jesus was rejected and crucified by the authorities, the disciples felt compelled to bear testimony to their experience of the risen Christ. This was how they could prove to their own people that Jesus was indeed the Messiah. And this they did with great courage. If Jesus was the Messiah, then the messianic age is to be ushered in shortly and people had to "save" themselves from the impending judgment by becoming part of this messianic age.

Peter gives the same message in the temple after the healing of the lame man:

> Fellow Israelites, why are you surprised at this and you stare at us... The God of Abraham, Isaac and Jacob, the God of our ancestors, has given divine glory to his servant Jesus. But you handed him over to the authorities... but God raised him from death – and we are witness to this... God announced long ago through all the prophets that his Messiah had to suffer... (3:12-13,15,18).

Apostolic preaching, in other words, was in many ways the continuation of the debate among the Jewish people on who Jesus was. The disciples were convinced that the new factor – Jesus' resurrection – should be witnessed to within this debate.

It is interesting that as late as in Acts 18, we read: "When Silas and Timothy arrived from Macedonia, Paul gave his whole time to preaching the message, testifying to the Jews that Jesus was the Messiah." This was in Corinth, and when those who disagreed with him got hold of Paul and brought him before the Governor of Achaia, Gallio, the governor saw this as a problem within the Jewish community. "Since it is an argument about words and names and your own law, you yourselves must settle it," he said, and drove them off from the court! (18:15-16).

To the end of the Acts of the Apostles, the narrative is marked by this controversy between those who believed in the resurrection of Jesus, and were therefore convinced that Jesus was the Messiah, and those who refused to believe it. The seeds of dissension were already there, for the Pharisees, including Paul, believed in the resurrection of the dead while the Sadducees did not. The matter was further complicated by the different expectations about the Messiah.

In the two fascinating accounts of Paul's defence of himself before Governor Felix (ch.24) and King Agrippa (ch.26), Paul speaks of his standing as a person within the Jewish community, and insists that the difficulties his opponents have with him have to do only with the resurrection faith about Jesus the Christ.

This is, however, only one side of the ministry of Paul. An early persecutor of those who "followed the way", once converted, Paul became a strong advocate for Jesus and the Way. When life became difficult in Jerusalem, he went to the Jewish communities scattered around Asia Minor. Almost in every instance he began his preaching in the local synagogue where the scattered Jewish communities regularly gathered for worship.

From the beginning he had a better response from the "Gentiles" who attended these synagogues than from the Jews who were divided over the question of messiahship and resurrection. From the beginning, therefore, there were "Gentiles" who responded to the apostolic preaching. These were, however, in most cases persons who were familiar with and inclined towards the Jewish faith. They were the "god-fearers", and for the most part they had heard the preaching at the synagogues which they regularly attended. In Thessalonica, for example, a number of Greeks believed in what Paul preached. But then they already knew something of the Jewish teaching through their regular attendance at the synagogue.

> According to his usual habit Paul went to the synagogue (in Thessalonica). There, during three sabbaths he held discussions with the people, quoting and explaining the (Jewish) scripture and proving from them that the Messiah had to suffer and rise from death. "This Jesus whom I announce to you", Paul said, "is the Messiah." Some of them were convinced and joined Paul and Silas; so did many of the leading women and a large group of Greeks who worshipped God (17:2-4).

Because of the increasing number of God-fearers or Gentiles who responded to Paul's preaching, he came to be known as the "Apostle to the Gentiles" and his mission came to be known as the "Gentile mission". But a careful reading of the Acts of the Apostles will show that Paul himself was most comfortable preaching to those who came out of, or were familiar with, the Jewish faith. Most of the Gentiles in Antioch and in Iconium who became believers, for example, had heard Paul speak to them on the Sabbath day in the synagogue (Acts 13,14).

This is of course not to deny that there were other converts than those who came from a Jewish background. Nor does it in any way discredit the importance of the fact that eventually the church did strike roots and grow in many new cultures.

All that we seek to show is that in the Acts of the Apostles there is a very specific Jewish context within which the kind of proclamation of the resurrection was seen by the apostles as the most appropriate form of witness. Most of those who listened to the witness of the Apostles were familiar with the expectations about the Messiah and what it meant to speak of Jesus as the Christ. The kind of passionate preaching and the attendant controversies were only to be expected. It will be wrong to assume that all this can be translated across other cultures and ages and the same methodology will serve as we relate and witness to Hindus, Buddhists, Muslims, etc. Here in the Acts we meet people who have an entirely different background. They see and understand the human predicament in very different ways from contemporary Muslims or Hindus.

But before we consider this problem we should stay with Paul for a little longer, and take a look at an aspect of his ministry which is not always highlighted in our reading of the Acts. Even though Paul's ministry led to discussion and controversy within his community, we cannot assume that he was an unsympathetic or uncompromising preacher who gave his message on a "take it or leave it" basis. In many places he spent a good deal of time in dialogue.

In Ephesus, for example, Paul is said to have led three months of discussions in the synagogue (19:8). Interestingly, the word "dialogue" is used to describe these conversations. And when the dialogue became too difficult in the synagogue, Paul moved to the lecture hall of Tyrannus where he continued to hold daily discussions for two whole years!

There is an interesting incident in Acts 17, where Paul is suddenly called upon to preach to a group of people who may be classified in a real sense as persons belonging entirely to another faith. This happens when Paul is waiting in Athens for Silas and Timothy to arrive.

He enters into conversation at the public square with those who are passing by, and almost accidentally gets the attention of the Epicurean and Stoic teachers who think that Paul is "showing off", talking about some foreign gods (see Acts 17:16-34 for a full account). The interest grows, and Paul finds himself called upon to speak to the city council.

It would appear that Paul was somewhat puzzled as to where he should begin. Perhaps for the first time, he is faced with a serious audience for whom the controversy over the Messiahship of Jesus has little or no relevance. Paul decides, therefore, to bear testimony to Jesus as the Risen One through whom God will "judge the whole world with justice" (v.31).

He has further problems. His audience does not share the Jewish world-view and they are not able to see the significance of Jesus within that framework either.

He makes the decision to begin where his listeners were in their own religious quest:

> I see that in every way you Athenians are very religious. For as I walked through your city and looked at the places where you worship, I found an altar on which is written 'To an Unknown God'. That which you worship, then, even though you do not know it, is what I now proclaim to you (vs.22-23).

Faced with an entirely non-Jewish audience, Paul is obliged to adopt a new method and a new idiom. He becomes theocentric in his approach. Quoting the verse, "We too are his children", from one of their poets, he speaks of himself and his hearers as children of the one God – "In him we live and move and exist" (v.28).

When he began to witness to Jesus' resurrection his audience became divided. Some expressed the desire to listen to him again, while to a number of people the whole concept appeared strange and even ridiculous. Some people, however, believed in what he said.

It has been said that Paul's attempt at dialogue in Athens was a misadventure. That is to say, the encounter was fruitless. Those who hold this view are convinced that Paul should have stuck to "straight preaching" even though his hearers did not have the background of Judaism.

It is of course difficult to imagine what would have happened if Paul had refused to enter into a dialogue with the religion of the people who listened to him, and had instead proclaimed

Jesus as the Christ, as he used to do in the synagogues. But I think that Paul confronted a real difficulty in Athens. It was not a misadventure, for Paul, like many of us today, was faced with a situation that was untypical of the rest of the encounters that he had had. For here, in a real sense, he was faced with people of other faiths. He was aware that neither the message nor the method he used in relating to those with a Jewish background was adequate to deal with this situation.

When he goes to the next city, Corinth, he returns to people of his own religious background!

The foregoing considerations are not meant to suggest that eventually there were no converts from those outside the Jewish faith perspective. We know there were. We know that soon the church lost its close relationship to the Jewish community and took deep roots in other cultures and became predominantly a "Gentile church". The process by which that happened was also a dialogic one, but that is outside our present scope.

The intention here is only to show the special nature of the material in the Acts of the Apostles and how both in its contents and method it related to a very specific situation.

When we read the Epistles of Paul, we find that the whole debate over Jesus had taken a fundamental shift. Since the church is now predominantly gentile, the emphasis on Jesus as the Messiah is no longer given prominence in the Epistles. Even though Jesus is called the Christ, a new meaning is given to the concept of Christ. Christ is no longer seen primarily as the Jewish Messiah but as the bearer of the grace of God, by faith in whom human persons are justified before God (Rom. 5).

Christ is seen as the one in whom God incarnated himself in the world (Phil. 2). Christ is the new man (1 Cor. 15); he reconciles God with human beings, he is the one who has paid the price of human sin (2 Cor. 5). Paul himself struggles in the Epistle to the Romans to carry on an inner dialogue with his own Jewish theology, seeking to find ways to relate his new faith to what he had inherited from his forebears.

Many of the exclusive claims made for Jesus must also be seen within this development. Sometimes they are made as part of the polemics against the Jewish community. Sometimes they arose as part of new confessions or understandings with regard to the significance of Christ.

Matthew, for example, quotes the Hebrew scriptures at every important point in his account of the life of Jesus, in order to prove that Jesus' life, death and resurrection were all part of God's overall plan. John interprets the life and teachings of Jesus to argue that Jesus is the true Messiah – the one sent by God to save God's people. Paul argues that the dispensation based on the Law has been brought to an end, and God has chosen in Jesus to save humankind by grace. The Apologetics reaches the peak in the Letter to the Hebrews where Jesus is interpreted as the one who replaces the whole religious institution of Israel!

There is no doubt that this growing understanding of the significance of Jesus by his followers is of the utmost importance for us. It is indeed part of the total tradition we have received as Christians. There are many aspects of it that speak meaningfully and forcefully to us today.

It is important, however, as we read the Bible, to recognize the nature of the material we have, and the specific circumstances that governed much that was said or done. We have seen how within the Bible itself there is a readiness to adopt, reinterpret and reject those things that make no sense in new situations. It would be totally misleading, for example, to argue that our relationship and witness today with people of other faiths should be modelled on the Acts of the Apostles. The tradition that began in the Acts of the Apostles is a living tradition. We will need to seek the nature of our obedience to Christ in our own times and in our own life with others.

6. Witnessing in dialogue

What does all this mean to the contemporary Christian witness to people of other faiths? Do we have a witness to offer? Is it legitimate to share the gospel? How do we go about it?

Let me begin with an incident that illustrates some of the issues.

For some years I was the minister of the Methodist Church in Jaffna, a town in the northern part of Sri Lanka. My home was near the municipal open-air theatre, intended for cultural events in the community. The theatre, however, was often rented by new church groups to organize evangelistic "crusades" – an insensitive and unimaginative way of describing Christian witness, common unfortunately even today. I had only to stand outside my gates to listen to the animated open-air preaching through loudspeakers, often by foreign visitors, ably interpreted into the local language.

In one such " crusade " the organizers decided to "mobilize" the local pastors and congregations. Next morning I had four visitors calling on me at home, inviting me and the congregation I served to become "part of the crusade".

I decided not to hide my displeasure at the way Hinduism was portrayed and attacked at the previous night's preaching, obviously based on an inadequate and very superficial grasp of its teachings.

Jaffna is a predominantly Hindu town. The relationships between Christians and Hindus had been carefully built and nurtured over decades. The Hindus respect the right of Christians to bear witness to their beliefs. But Christian witness should build community and not disrupt it. We should respect the fact that Hinduism is a vital and living religion and that we have much to learn from it. Our witness has to be an encounter of commitments in which we share our faith with them. I spoke along these lines.

The visitors were surprised and looked at me with some suspicion. "Are we not under the command to preach the gospel and to make disciples of all nations?" asked one of them, reminding me of the great missionary commission in Matthew 28:18. "Jesus also commissioned his disciples to be his witnesses in Jerusalem, in all Judea, Samaria and to the ends of the earth," said the foreign preacher in the team. To anyone from the USA, Jaffna would certainly look like the ends of the earth.

The local pastor reminded me of St Paul's words: "Woe unto me if I do not preach the gospel."

It was a reasonably friendly conversation on how to bear witness to Hindu neighbours, but I remained unconvinced to the end about joining the "crusade". After a prayer, which reminded us of the "urgency to preach the gospel to perishing generations", the team left my home.

This was a painful experience. For I deeply believed in witnessing, and yet had to turn down an invitation to participate in witnessing. I have returned to this incident many times when reflecting on Christian witness.

One of my difficulties had to do with taking the famous passage in Matthew 28 as the basic rationale for witnessing. Biblical scholars have problems with this passage, for the trinitarian formula would suggest that the particular formulation comes from the early church, and not from Jesus himself. For even in the Acts of the Apostles, the disciples baptized the believers in the name of Jesus and not in the name of the Trinity. That came later.

My difficulty, however, did not arise from problems concerning the authenticity of the passage. I had a far more fundamental problem. Do Christians bear witness to Jesus Christ because they are under a command or a commission to do so? Do Christians go about converting and baptizing others because Christ has asked them to do so? This was the problem I had with the group that met in my home.

We meet this argument all the time. Every time one speaks about dialogue with people of other faiths someone would invariably bring up the question of the Great Commission in Matthew 28. "But are we not under an obligation to bear witness? Jesus has commissioned us to make disciples of nations, baptizing them in the name of the Father, the Son and the Holy Spirit", they would say.

Much of the crisis in Christian witness has to do with the fact that it is done for the wrong reasons. Is it not true that many Christians are more convinced about their own responsibility to be witnesses than about the need of others to hear the gospel? Is it not a fact that a number of "crusades" are arranged out of a sense of duty and not because we care? It is not because the organizers know and love the people whom they address, and want to share their lives with them, but because they wish to fulfill the mandate to preach the gospel and make disciples.

How can we allow Christian witness to arise out of self-interest and a sense of obligation or self-fulfilment? A rereading of the scriptures, especially of the account of the ministry of Jesus, shows that the biblical understanding of witness is quite different. It has to do with incarnation, with self-giving, with setting up the signs of the kingdom, with accepting those who are not acceptable to others, of sharing our lives.

There are of course other models, as in the specific situation in the Acts, where the disciples bear witness to the resurrection to a community that had lived through, or at least heard of, the crucifixion of Jesus.

The rationale people give for witnessing is often revealing. Gandhi, for example, took the Sermon on the Mount as one of the bases for his mission among the people, and he subjected himself to the discipline involved in the teaching to which he bore witness.

One problem in making the Great Commission the basis of Christian mission is that all kinds of people without either the right or the spiritual candour to give witness set themselves up as persons who have been commanded to give witness. Here witness becomes counter-witness.

Another difficulty has to do with "making disciples" which is often equated with conversion in the sense of moving from one religious community to another.

The Bible, by and large, talks about believers, not about converts. In Jesus' own ministry, people did not have to move from one community to another, but from a self-centred life to a God-centred life. Repentance had to do with a radical renewal of relationship with God and one's neighbours. Jesus preached that God's kingly rule has come into our lives and challenged people to order their lives according to its values. He showed no anxiety to convert people from Judaism and to set up a rival community.

It is of course true that a number of persons took up discipleship, called themselves by his name, and after the resurrection the church became a historical reality. But can we say that the gospel message or the fact that believers became an identifiable community provides a biblical basis to speak of others as "unreached millions"? "Unreached by whom?" asks Stanley

Samartha in one of his essays; the fact that the preacher has not reached a place or spoken to a people does not mean that God has not reached them. On what basis can we speak of the people of other faiths as "those who have not come to the light"?

Of course one is aware that these attitudes are not characteristic of all persons who are engaged in evangelism, or in all efforts to preach the gospel to large numbers of persons. This is by no means an argument against Christian witness. Such witness is wholly legitimate; it arises out of a profound spirituality that fills our life as we encounter Christ. That cries out to be shared, but it can only be shared in humility.

All that we seek to show is that there is also a strong biblical basis for a new context for Christian witness, namely, the context of dialogue. It is rooted in the Bible insofar as it is expressed in the life and ministry of Jesus himself.

Not that dialogue is a new tool for mission or that one engages in dialogue in order to manipulate others. It simply means that witness can and does happen in dialogue. The WCC's *Guidelines on Dialogue* puts it this way:

> ...we do not see dialogue and giving of witness as standing in any contradiction to each other. Indeed, as Christians enter dialogue with their commitment to Jesus Christ, time and again the relationship of dialogue gives opportunity for authentic witness. Thus... we feel able with integrity to commend the way of dialogue as one in which Jesus Christ can be confessed in the world today; at the same time we feel able with integrity to assure our partners in dialogue that we come not as manipulators but as genuine fellow-pilgrims, to speak with them of what we believe God to have done in Jesus Christ who has gone before us, but whom we seek to meet anew in dialogue.[1]

What then is the spirit in which we can bear Christian witness which is biblical and at the same time authentic?

Some time ago my colleague in the WCC who publishes the Monthly Letter on Evangelism asked me to write a letter to a Christian in Sri Lanka who wishes to be a witness to the Hindus. I wrote the following letter. It is an attempt to articulate how Christian witness can still be offered in our time, but in an attitude and spirit that respect our neighbour as a child of God.

---

[1] 1979, p.11.

"Dear Ranjith,

"You have asked me to give you some advice on bearing witness to Christ among your Hindu neighbours. The Hindus believe that anyone who has an experience of spiritual truth has the right to share it with others. They, therefore, do not object to authentic witness. It is important that this trust and openness to witness should not be used for manipulation of one religion by another, but for a genuine sharing of religious experience and truth as we have come to perceive it. It is in this spirit that I put down some of my own thoughts on this matter.

"I am pleased to know that your interest in witness arises from deep convictions about Christ which have actually fashioned your own life. Why do I make a special point of this? There are some Christians who would argue that evangelism is based on the 'command' to preach the gospel. They would say that the validity of the gospel message is not dependent on the preacher and that the message has its own effectiveness.

"This is not the place to argue the theological validity or otherwise of such a position. But I know that the Hindus will not separate the preacher from the message, the evangelist from the gospel, the truth from its manifestation. This arises from a long-established Indian tradition that only a person who has had a spiritual experience can have authority to impart it to others. 'Can anyone recommend to others what has not been profoundly true to oneself?' they would ask. 'And, how can we believe what is said, unless we see its effects on the one who says it?'

"That is why doctrinal claims about Christ, or belief statements on what God has done in Christ, leave the Hindus unimpressed, even though they have a great respect for Christ as a spiritual leader. Anyone who wishes to witness to Hindus should not ignore the long-established Indian tradition that the person and the message he or she gives cannot be separated. This is a simple but profound rule of the thumb used in India – if it is a good message, it must be both heard and seen!

"I know that many Christians have problems with this attitude. They would want to separate the message from the messenger and want to preserve the integrity of the message itself. But this is not a 'selective treatment' that the Hindus give to the Christian preachers. In their own history they have always applied this principle to distinguish truth from error. This is how

Hinduism functions as a living religion without a centralized authority to lay down the essentials and the limits of what they should believe. Instead of reacting too quickly to this attitude, you should ponder very deeply about it, relating it to our own Christian history. Perhaps we must also meditate on Christ's invitation to the disciples in Acts 1, where the emphasis is on 'you shall *be* my witnesses'.

"For the same reason, witness to the Hindus can never be based on any prior absolute claims about Christ. Such claims hinder rather than help Christian witness. Let me give an example. A preacher stands in front of a Hindu and proclaims: 'Christ is the only way; there is no salvation except through him.' However sincere and well-meaning the preacher may be, the Hindu will consider him or her as being both intolerant and arrogant. Why? They see in such a statement an implicit refusal to consider any other way. This they consider as intolerance. More seriously, such a statement or such claims preclude and deny anything others may have to say on this subject, even without giving a hearing to it. Nothing hurts the Hindus more. They cannot even understand why Christians have to say such a thing. This does not mean that the Hindu denies the witness of the preacher. They would admit that this may be profoundly true for the preacher. Christ to him or her may have become the 'only way'. But they would argue that such a statement has no validity outside the preacher's own experience and conviction. It becomes true once again only when another person comes to the same conviction for himself or herself, and is able to experience and see Christ as *the way*. This may appear to be an artificial distinction to some Christians. But this has a very important bearing on witness to the Hindus. They believe that the hearer should *recognize* the truth and should not be forced to accept it.

"If you ask me to single out one factor that has been the greatest hindrance to genuine witness, I would say that it is these absolute claims that some Christians make for Christ. The decisiveness of Christ must be a matter of experience and should never be the subject of preaching.

"Again, some of the evangelists behave as though they are bringing God for the first time to the Hindus. The Hindus are amazed at such an idea. To begin with, how can God be 'taken' anywhere? The whole creation lives and moves in God. God's own witness has never been absent at any time or in any place. More importantly, the Hindus have a spiritual tradition reaching back over four thousand years of seeking to understand the mystery of life and its relation to God. Within it there is every shade of theological opinion; a variety of philosophical reflections on God ranging from atheism to strict monotheism. Many modes of relating to God have been tested over centuries – meditation, good works, yoga, the way of devotion, the way of love. Much more importantly, there have been within the Hindu tradition great spiritual giants whose experience of God, spiritual excellence, and life totally devoted to God's service can neither be denied nor ignored. To know Hinduism and the Hindus at their best is a humbling experience to any Christian. Here we are confronted with a living spiritual tradition tested and tried over centuries, within which there is an undeniable experiencing of God's grace and love.

"Faced with this reality, what can an evangelist do? Some simply deny that this spiritual tradition has any validity at all. They would say that the whole matter is a 'human' attempt and that Hindus can never have the actual knowledge of God until they know God through Christ. Others choose simply to ignore the whole thing. They pretend that the Hindus have had no spiritual history behind them, and behave as though the world was born only yesterday!

"'What does this mean?' you would ask. 'Are you not arguing that Hindus do not need the gospel? Are you not, by implication, saying that there is nothing new that you can take to the Hindu as Christian witness?'

"That is a valid question, but the real challenge to witness also lies in that question. The Hindus already have some of the loftiest ideals any religion can offer. If you want to engage in witness to the Hindus, therefore, you should think very deeply about this and know why you want to witness to them. And, whatever you offer as witness should be credible insofar as it is seen to be true to your own experience, and should have been seen by the Hindu to answer specific questions one has about one's life and destiny. That is why it is important to know them personally and to share our message in ways that make sense to them, and answer the questions that they ask. If we frame both the questions and the answers how can there be any effective witness? Please look up the many ways in which Christ dealt with people.

"As I have said at the beginning, there are no basic problems in offering witness to Hindus, because Hinduism is an open-ended religion able to consider, test and incorporate any spiritual experience that may prove to be beneficial to human-kind. Precisely because of this openness, it also would reject any meaningless claims that are not backed by actual spiritual experience.

"Apart from these points, which in a sense can also apply to any witness situation, there are some specific matters you should remember. These concern the thought-patterns in which the Hindu operates.

"In the Bible the human predicament is depicted in the framework of 'sin-fall and alienation from God'. Many of the ways we understand the significance of Christ speak to this framework. A good example is the understanding of Jesus as the Christ – the Messiah. The concept and all that it means were well understood within Judaism and the church that was evolving out of it.

"But the Hindus understand the human predicament within an entirely different framework, using such concepts as Karma, rebirth, cycles of life-processes, etc. How do they perceive the human condition? In what way can the good news become incarnate within this tradition? These are points worth ponder-ing. There are some who feel that this is an unnecessary preoccupation. 'All people are alienated from God; they are in sin; and what is needed is the direct presentation of the gospel,' they would say. You should consider whether this is really so. The Hindu religion, culture and belief are so entrenched in the Indian heart and mind, that it is difficult to imagine a Hindu who does not operate on the above thought-form consciously or otherwise.

"Let me mention just one more point. This relates to the presentation of the gospel and the expectation on how it should be received. Some evangelists think that the gospel message is a 'package-deal'. They would insist that Christ and all that Christians have come to believe about him (Saviour, Son of God, Redeemer, etc.) should be accepted by the hearers. Often this package includes baptism and church membership. In an earlier age, this also included a change of name, dress and culture! If you want to witness to Christ to a Hindu, you should first get over the 'package' idea.

"The Hindus would accept Christ as a great teacher, guru, saint, etc., and one should never attempt to enforce one's own understanding on them. It is of interest that even Christ's disciples had various perceptions about who Christ was, and they grew in their own understanding with the passage of time. What is wrong with it? Let Christ be to them whoever he will be to them. The 'package' concept was among the factors that alienated Mahatma Gandhi from Christianity as a religion.

"Let me conclude with a word on our attitude to the act of witnessing itself. The most important lesson I have learned from the ministry of Christ is the great integrity with which he approached people. The Hindu is not an object for conversion. He or she is a fellow-pilgrim with whom we share the decisive impact Christ has had on our own lives. Even as we do so, we should be prepared to listen to any witness he or she may have to offer to us. Their lives may be greatly enriched by our witness. Similarly, we may be enabled to see the unsearchable riches of God through their witness to us.

"In such a witness situation a Hindu may recognize a challenge to Christian discipleship which he or she may want to accept openly in freedom. On the other hand, the Hindu may see no reason why he or she has to make such an open commitment of discipleship to Christ.

"Can you, in both circumstances, accept the Hindu as your brother or sister who stands, like you, within the unfathomable love and grace of God?

"If you can, then you have received the spiritual maturity to be a witness of Christ to the Hindu.

"Love, Wesley"

The letter was an attempt to place Christian witness within the context of dialogue, and to show that an open and genuine relationship with people who live by other faith traditions is in no way contrary to the biblical faith. Nor is our willingness to listen and learn from others.

It should be admitted, however, that in the context of our new attitude to religious pluralism one should highlight some of the biblical themes that have not played a central role in the church's self-understanding in the past. The recovery of these would provide a theological basis that will make dialogue the natural Christian way of life in religiously plural situations. It is to these we turn in our final chapter.

7. Towards a theology of dialogue

You would have noticed that I have been emphasizing one or another side of the scriptures, and have been selective in referring to biblical passages in my attempt to plead for a new way of relating to people of other faiths. It is of course possible for another person to select other parts of the scriptures, or to favour another interpretation of a passage, in order to argue for a traditional or yet another way of approaching the question. I admitted in the introduction to this book that here there is no argument to be won. All that one can hope to do is to show that there is another side – which in my view is central to the spirit of the biblical message – which supports and calls us to a life of dialogue.

It must be noted, however, that no view, however traditional, conservative or long-standing, can claim to be "biblical" in the sense of embodying a definitive and inclusive teaching of the Bible. All views on this and similar questions are based on a selective approach to the Bible. The selection of verses, passages and emphases is often guided by the historical situation, spiritual maturity, cultural conditioning, and the specific issues faced by the person who seeks the biblical message. One only needs to look at the history of the interpretation of specific issues – such as the question of the Christian attitude to war, Christian involvement in politics, or the place of women in church and society – to realize how the Bible can be approached in many different ways. The historical situation of the church has often shaped or changed the way in which biblical passages are selected, interpreted and applied to daily life.

This does not of course mean that the Bible has no original or central message to give, and that people are free to draw their own conclusions from it. Throughout history, and even today, all kinds of unjust causes have claimed to receive the support of biblical authority. Apartheid in South Africa is by no means an isolated example.

No one can claim to have a monopoly on "truth as revealed in the scriptures". There is a critical and dialectical relationship between the witness offered in the Bible and the reader who brings the experience of the community to bear on that message. One must of course be honest to listen to the message that emerges from this encounter. It is most important that the community of faith is able to discern the result as the guidance of scripture. This has always been the safeguard against individual interpretations that do violence to the central message of the scripture.

The Bible is not a static book of laws which gives specific guidance on every issue faced by the community. Itself an account of the struggle of a faith community, the Bible is a book with which we must struggle. It is this that makes the Bible a living word and not a dead letter.

Many Christians, however, commonly believe that the Bible has in it the unalterable "substance" of our faith which we must accept without question. I have often heard people argue that our attitude to people of other faiths "should be based on the biblical teaching", or that "the biblical truths should be the standard by which we judge the validity or otherwise of other truth claims".

If one were to examine this and ask which biblical teaching or truth is being referred to here, one finds that the argument is based on a verse here or there, or on a statement Paul or Peter had made in a specific context. It is common experience that those who speak about the "biblical truth" or the "biblical message" are actually referring to a particular verse or verses which have become the basis of their own perception of an issue. If one were to quote another verse or other verses of the Bible to show another perspective, one immediately gets caught in the problem of selection, interpretation and emphasis.

The Bible, as we have seen, is a story of faith and faithfulness. Here we have a story of two communities, Israel and the church, struggling to understand and put into practice their commitment to God. We have the story of how these two communities also celebrate the faithfulness of God. It is a fascinating and spiritually enriching account of the pilgrimage of faith of those who have gone before us.

For Christians, it is also more than a spiritually enriching book, for here we find the first and earliest records of the life and teachings of Jesus as selected, arranged and interpreted by his followers. Similarly here we also have an account of the birth and the growth of the Christian community, and some of the ways in which persons like John, Paul, Peter and the author of the Letter to the Hebrews struggled to interpret the significance of Jesus to the communities to which they related.

What is most important is to recognize this "struggle-to-understand", to which the Bible bears witness. Those who treat the Bible as having some kind of static authority do not respect this important witness of the scriptures. Let me illustrate.

The Council at Jerusalem

Jesus and most of his immediate followers were Jews and, as we have seen, even after the resurrection experience, the disciples continued to go to the temple, and saw themselves as part of the Jewish tradition.

But the expanding ministry, primarily of Paul and Barnabas, brought into this community those who were not part of the Jewish tradition – the "Gentiles". The church was faced with a new situation, for the Gentiles did not keep the Law, which was obligatory for the Jews, and were not circumcized, which was the mark of belonging to the covenant community.

Acts 15 is the story of how the church struggled with this new situation. The questions that came up had far-reaching implications. Was it important to preserve the Christian roots in Judaism and, if so, how much of Judaism was to be accepted in order to be faithful to the tradition out of which the church was growing? Could circumcision, the sign of belonging to the covenant community, be so easily given up? Was the Torah to become part of the Christian heritage?

These were very difficult questions, indeed, and of course there was at that time no New Testament to provide its authority. Acts 15 does not give the details of what must have been a difficult, emotionally charged and divisive debate. There were no ready-made answers and there were strong reasons, with vocal advocates, to present both sides of the argument.

Finally the community arrived at a decision. The "Gentile" Christians need not accept circumcision, and they need not be required to keep the Law. They should however abstain from food-habits and social behaviour that will make it difficult for Christians of Jewish origin to have fellowship with them.

Here, in the Bible itself, we have the story of how the community of faith was prepared to reconsider and reformulate its stance when faced with a new situation. It was a difficult decision, but it had to be made.

This painful inner dialogue within the church opened it up to a whole new reality. It radically transformed both the nature and the life of the Christian community.

In many ways, Acts 15 prefigures what is likely to become an equally painful and divisive debate in the latter part of the twentieth century, namely, the Christian response to religious pluralism. Here again what the church will decide will have far-reaching consequences for its life and theology.

The challenge of religious pluralism

The church has from the very beginning lived in the context of other faiths. What was part of Judaism soon came into direct contact with the religion, culture and philosophy of the Graeco-Roman world. These contacts influenced the formulation and interpretation of the Christian faith. We see this already within the Bible. Paul uses many metaphors – redemption, salvation, reconciliation, atonement, re-creation, etc. – to understand the significance of the death of Christ. John, as we have already seen, turns to the Wisdom tradition of the *logos* to speak of Jesus as the pre-existent creative word of God, a concept that had strong parallels in Greek thought.

The subsequent history of theology is the story of how the various philosophical and cultural contacts of the church enriched and expanded the theological traditions already present in the Bible. In all these developments the church's contact with other religions and cultures has played an important role.

Today the church is faced with a situation which is essentially new. For in the past the contact with other faiths had primarily the effect of enriching and expanding the Christian faith, but always the church had a self-understanding because of which it refused to take the other faiths with the seriousness they deserved. The church's theology was at the service of its missiology. The theology and philosophy of religion that came out of the church's tradition were always *apologetic* in the final analysis; they always showed why the Christian faith was superior to the other faiths. Much of this was also aided by the power relationship between people professing the Christian faith and those of other faiths. Both under Constantine and more recently under colonial rule – the two periods when the church took roots in different cultures in a big way – the other faiths had no opportunity to challenge the Christian faith forcefully and radically.

Today we have indeed a new situation, and it is important to note some of the characteristics of this new stage in human history.

First, the other religious traditions have recovered from their colonial subjugation, and present themselves as universal alternatives to the Christian faith. There has been a resurgence of religions during the last few decades. There is a new vitality about them, and a new missionary zeal. The confidence that some day the Christian faith would replace all other religions, as a historical reality and not only as an eschatological consummation, has been waning. The empires have fallen; so have the ambitions of the religious traditions that went with them.

Second, these religious traditions have made so many inroads into even the "Christian" West that religious pluralism has become a reality in almost every society. Today there are more Muslims in France than there are Reformed Christians, and more Muslims in Britain than Methodists. Religions are no longer in far-off lands. Further, the minority churches that live in the midst of other faith communities are under much pressure to rethink their own attitudes to and relationships with their neighbours. They are becoming more and more convinced that they must seek and build truly human communities with them. They are convinced that they can no longer find answers to the problems of life all by themselves. For good or for ill, a large number of communities will need to come together in order to work for common goals and achieve tangible results.

Third, and perhaps most important, there is a developing discovery of the riches of other faiths. At one time, Buddhism was considered to be "pagan" because it did not pay attention to a doctrine of God. Hinduism was often dismissed as idol worship and superstition. Today Christians show much interest in Buddhist meditation and Hindu Yoga. At one time the Muslims were looked upon as rivals; today there is growing interest in the Islamic understanding of community and prayer. One can go on adding to this list.

There are some who frown upon the current Christian interest in Buddhism, Hinduism and Islam. My purpose is not to go into the reasons for this new interest nor to evaluate it. All I want to emphasize is that there is a new awareness of religious pluralism, not as a threatening reality to be rejected, but as a reality to come to terms with.

That is to say, the theological hostility or neutrality towards other faiths is no longer tenable. The past models within which Christians sought to accommodate the other faiths can no longer suffice. There is new wine, and we need new wine-skins.

There are those who claim that all this arises from the "loss of nerve" that the churches experience in the present post-colonial period. They would say that what we need is a "new confidence" and that we should "rally our forces" and engage in an "intensive mission in the six continents".

But can we not see this as a new historical moment in the life of the church, which could give it a new impetus and mark a new beginning? Can we not say that the church is being called to deal *theologically* with religious pluralism and to come to a new understanding of the way to relate to, live and work with people of other faiths?

The Council of Jerusalem, described in Acts 15, could have taken a much more cautious stand. They could have rejected outright the need to deal with pluralism within the church. It could certainly have decided to preserve its Jewishness. It could have decided that, for good or ill, all those who wished to be part of the Christian community had to undergo circumcision and keep the Law of Moses. In many ways such a decision would have left the church with a manageable and more uniform community and theology. But the open-ended inner dialogue within the church resulted in a decision that totally changed the character of the church. Are we not, as churches, in a similar situation today with regard to religious pluralism?

We cannot of course draw too many parallels between Acts 15 and today's situation. The details differ. But what is important is to note that the church was open to the "new" and the unknown future, and the churches today should be willing to be inspired by this attitude.

What we are saying is that the time has come for the church to struggle to discover a new theological basis for its relationship with people of other faith convictions. It should be a theological basis that enables the Christian to be committed to Christ, and yet be open to the witness of others. It should enable the Christian to joyfully witness to his or her convictions and yet feel free to discern God's kingdom at work in other lives. It has to be a theological basis that can create genuine caring communities across all barriers; communities that are able to work together for justice and peace for all.

Is there, in the Bible, a basis for such a theology? That is not an easy question to answer. For the Bible does not deal with questions for which the community of faith should find answers as it struggles with the meaning of its commitment to Jesus Christ in new situations. At the same time, the Christian community today stands in a relationship to the Bible and to the theological tradition that has been developed down the centuries – which give it its identity. Theology, therefore, is not the opinions of individual persons. The theologian reflects on behalf of the community of faith, and it is the community of faith that should recognize the validity and relevance of what is said – whether in fact it is in tune with the faith handed down the centuries. The task of the theologian is to point to those areas in which he or she sees the need for new obedience. Or it may be only a call to emphasize anew aspects of the faith that have always been there both in scripture and tradition but have not been isolated and held up because of specific historical situations.

What are some of the areas in which a theology that seeks to take religious pluralism and interfaith dialogue seriously will need to concentrate? During the last several years many theologians have been working in this area. Let me point to some of the aspects where attention will need to be given in the coming years.

Towards a theocentric approach to theology

There are many voices that criticize the virtual Christomonism of Protestant theology. This is seen to be at the root of much of the Protestant inability to deal with religious pluralism. The apostles witnessed to their faith that God has revealed himself in a special way in Jesus Christ. Some branches of theology have taken this faith and, based on a selective treatment of the scriptures, developed it into the claim that Christ is the "full", "final", "ultimate", and "decisive" revelation of God.

In missionary situations, the claim is often made that there is no other "true" revelation of God and, even if there were, they are so partial that it is only through Christ that we can have any "real" knowledge of God.

To this is added the "exclusive verses" of the Bible as statements of truth: "No one comes to the Father, except through me", and "There is no other name in which salvation is given."

What emerges is a situation where God is completely pushed to the periphery, and Christianity, at least in its Protestant missionary activity, provides no basis to relate to people who live by other faiths. All that one can do within this understanding is to appeal to those of other faiths to accept Jesus Christ as their Lord. Missiology becomes the total context of relationships.

A little reflection will show that this attitude is in many ways inconsistent with the overall teaching of the Bible. It is God who is at the centre of the biblical message; yes, the God who is the creator of all and in whom all have their being. The story of Israel is the story of how this community constantly experienced God's presence with them in a loving and saving way.

When we turn to the story of Jesus, one is constantly amazed by the theocentric life that he lived. He did not claim to be the full, final and decisive revelation of God, and it is difficult to see how such an exclusive position can be taken even on the basis of the Johanine verse, "He who has seen me has seen the Father."

Jesus' life, let us recall, was lived in constant reference to God. At his death he committed his life to the Father; after the resurrection he claimed that he was going to the Father. The whole of his teaching is based on the kingdom of God.

Much of Protestant theology does only lip-service even to the doctrine of Trinity. It is Jesus, fortunately, who taught us the "Our Father", which urges us to place our life in the hands of God.

The recovery of a theocentric theology will enable Christians, without denying their witness to Jesus Christ, to stand alongside people of other faiths as children of the one God.

Such a theo-centric approach does not necessarily give the theological framework for dialogue with people who live by other faith convictions. Buddhists, for example, have a conception of reality within which the Christian conception of God has little relevance. Theocentric understanding is, therefore, not a new framework we thrust on others. Rather it helps us as Christians to make theological sense of our life with others within our faith-commitment.

It is only from a theocentric view that one can respect the faith of Abraham and the obedience of Moses. At the same time it will help Christians to recognize that the biblical story is the story of one people among many, all of whom are within God's providence. It will enable Christians to be ready to listen to others and to discern the ways in which God has blessed other lives and acted in other ways.

This does not of course mean that now the Christian will accept everything as the activity of God or that he or she has no way by which to discern what belongs to God's kingdom and what does not. To be a Christian is to show one's readiness to discern the world from the standpoint of faith in Jesus Christ. But this will be done in the perspective of a wider understanding of God's relationship with the world. It will certainly rule out at least the *a priori* assumption that what does not come as a result of faith in Jesus Christ cannot be of God!

We must recognize that such an emphasis does not in any way mark a departure from the central message of the Bible; rather, it is a corrective that will enable Christians to live in a religiously plural world, without denying their own specific calling and at the same time making theological sense of the life and experience of others who share their lives with them.

Rethinking Christology

But what of our witness to Christ? Is it not our belief about Christ that makes us Christians? Is not Christology the central issue of Christian relationship with other faiths?

It is indeed so. To be a Christian is to become a disciple of Christ, believing in the meaning and significance of his life for ours. Christian witness has to do with our witness to Christ and his message.

The question here, however, is about the nature of this belief and the kind of witness that arises from it. Much of what passes for biblical Christology is a result of the attempts of Paul to understand the significance of Jesus and his resurrection in its relation to Jewish Law and other institutions. It is a struggle that he as a Jew had to carry on in order to make theological sense of his new commitment. As we have seen in the chapter dealing with the Acts of the Apostles, the initial attempt was to understand Jesus as the Messiah promised by the prophets.

When the church became predominantly Gentile, as we noted earlier, the emphasis on the Messiahship was gradually given up even though the title Christ was retained.

Jesus' divinity and sonship on the one hand, and an understanding of him as the New Adam on the other became more appropriate in the gentile environment. We can see this development in the letters written by Paul to different congregations. In later history, Christology became preoccupied with the questions of the divinity and humanity of Jesus, a struggle that led to much controversy and division within the church.

We can no longer frame the Christological question in terms of the divine-human controversy or reduce our enquiry to an exploration of whether or how the Godhead was present in the person of Jesus.

The Bible itself does not have a definitive Christology. We have only an account of the growing awareness among the followers of Jesus that they were confronted here not simply with a historical person or a historical event but someone whose life, death and resurrection had a profound meaning for them. And the story of the New Testament letters is the struggle to expound this meaning in terms of their own faith and within the limits of the religion and culture of their time.

If Christians believe that Jesus became a "window into God", then the witness to Christ has to do with the nature of God that we see through his life. If Christians also believe that the Christ-event has a salvic significance for the whole of humanity, it has to be witnessed to as a claim of faith. We cannot use this faith-claim as a basis to deny other claims of faith. However true our own experience, however convinced we are about a faith-claim, it has to be given as a claim of faith and not as truth in the absolute sense.

There is indeed no reason why one should develop a Christology which stands on the negative premise that there is "no other revelation", "no other way", "no other salvation", etc. One can only witness to what one knows and not to what one does not know. Even the most convinced Christian can only witness in humility and in terms of his or her convictions, for truth is beyond the grasp of any human being.

Religious pluralism does not require that one covers up one's witness for the sake of mutual respect and understanding. Indeed, it is the one who has a witness to offer that will contribute to the richness of a pluralistic community. But such a witness should be given in the spirit of humility, and there should be the readiness to listen to and learn from the witness of others. And for this we need to develop a Christology which will place before people the demands of the kingdom.

Once, returning from Asia, I had a young person from Europe sitting next to me in the plane. From his appearance I could make out that he had been to India and, like so many young people in the West, on a religious quest. I decided to have a conversation with him and asked him what had taken him to India.

He was very open. "I was a Christian as you could have easily guessed", he said, "and my Christianity taught me that I had been saved and that I should help bring others to Christ. Somehow this did not appeal to me. I am much more challenged by the God-ward devotion of Hinduism and the teaching of self-denial in Buddhism."

As a Christian minister myself, I was a little disturbed. It may be that this particular young man did not have a good grasp of the Christian faith. But for me, it was the teaching ministry of the church that seemed to stand under judgment. How was it that this young man never came to know that at the centre of the Christian faith is self-denial and a life fully turned towards God? Have our Christological doctrines obscured the Jesus of the Bible so much that this young man could not even recognize in him someone who challenged people to live a radically new life? I was not offended because he had been to India. I was wondering whether in God's providence this person was being led to some of the essentials of his own religious tradition through an encounter with other faiths.

The more I reflected on the event the more I was convinced that the Christologies we have in the Bible are signposts. They show how the early disciples and apostles struggled to understand the significance of Jesus for their lives and times.

In the new context of religious pluralism we cannot ignore our own responsibility to continue that struggle. The biblical witness beckons us to this task.

God's reign and God's mission

Much of our difficulty in relating to religious pluralism also has to do with an ecclesio-centric theology. We should not forget that at least in some stage in history "No salvation outside Christ" became "No salvation outside the church"! The Christian community is always under the temptation to look upon itself as the "saved community" as against the "unsaved world". Such an understanding, expressed or unexpressed, has distorted and vitiated the church's relationship with people of other faiths.

The new situation demands more sustained efforts to recover the kingdom or the reign of God as the focus of Christian theology. Many attempts in the past to bring the kingdom to the centre of theology were short-lived. The church-centred theology has always prevailed.

The concept of God's kingly rule opens up all kinds of new possibilities for relationships. For the kingdom knows no bounds, and it can only be known by its signs. No one knows the times and seasons God has set to bring the kingdom to its fulfilment and no one but God, who knows the secrets of human hearts, knows who belongs to the kingdom and who does not.

More importantly, the emphasis on the kingdom will also result in the emphasis on the Spirit, who moves where the Spirit wills. The Spirit touches the hearts of people and takes hold of situations in unknown ways, thus opening up the possibility to discern God's activity in all kinds of places and in all sorts of lives.

A re-emphasis on the Spirit of God as the One who moves, corrects and rules over all life will open up many possibilities for relationship with people of other faiths.

Perhaps the most important task is to reconceive the biblical concept of the "Mission of God" as the basis of our relationship with others.

One often speaks about "Christian mission" or "church's mission". The whole of the Bible relates to only one mission – the mission of God. All other missions have to find their place within it. The Christian witness to Christ, the Christian service to humanity and Christian acts of worship are all only a part of – and participation in – the overall mission of God, which knows no boundaries. It is the conscious or unconscious equation of Christian mission with God's mission that makes it impossible for Christians to relate to the signs of the kingdom which they discern outside the Christian community. The conviction that we as Christians are only a part of a larger mission of God will enable us to join hands and work with people of other faiths in a more conscious way.

This will also help the church to rediscover its own role as the servant community, and not as one whose presence threatens others.

I once participated in a German-Thai (Christian-Buddhist) dialogue meeting in Bad Boll. A Thai girl, who was a silent listener to the dialogue for three days, came up, on the last day, much to the surprise of many, to make some comments. "This meeting has taken me by surprise," she said, "and I am very pleased with it. For I always thought that the only reason that Christians showed any interest in Buddhists was to make them Christians."

It was a rewarding moment. For here was one person whose impression of the church as a threatening presence had been changed, and she had come to experience the Christian community as a caring presence. But to the majority of people of other faiths, the church and its mission continue to be a threat, for however loving that mission is, it is seen to have the aim of overpowering and replacing the faiths of others. "Two thousand years of Christian love", said a person of another faith, "is enough to make anybody nervous"!

It is almost impossible to speak about Christian mission in this way without being accused of denying the relevance of Christian witness. Religious pluralism, let me repeat, does not demand that people give up or hide the witness they have to offer. But it certainly demands that such witness is given in the spirit of one who has truly experienced the humility, the vulnerability and the self-giving that are at the centre of Christ's own witness. Such a witness can only be given in the context of a larger vision of the mission of God in which we are partners and fellow-pilgrims with all others who also stand within the grace and love of God. Thus, even as we witness, we listen to the witness of others.

I am aware that there is nothing very new in what I have said, for throughout the church's history people from time to time have called the church to a more inclusive understanding of the community in which it lives and of which it is a part. But this has become far more urgent today, for religious pluralism is here to stay, and we will need to find theological bases and spiritual resources to accept and affirm the whole realm of human life as the arena of God's love and activity.

That will not happen if we use the Bible as a dividing wall between one community and another. The Bible, on the other hand, should be seen as the light or the lamp that sheds light and illumination on the life of Christians as they seek to live with people of other faiths. There is in the Bible a more open, generous and inclusive understanding of God and God's ways than we seem to be aware of. There is in the Bible a teaching that will free us from the self and enable us to live in community with others.

And the theology we need, as Stanley Samartha said in his book *Courage for Dialogue*, is one "that is not less but more true to God by being generous and open, a theology not less but more loving towards the neighbour by being friendly and willing to listen, a theology that does not separate us from our fellow human beings but supports us in our common struggles and hopes. As we live together with our neighbours, what we need today is a theology that refuses to be impregnable but which, in the spirit of Christ, is both ready and willing to be vulnerable."